Awakening Inner Guru

AWAKENING INNER GURU

THE PATH OF REALIZING GOD WITHIN

By

BANANI RAY AND AMIT RAY

Inner Light Publishers
www.inner-light-in.com

Published by:

INNER LIGHT PUBLISHERS
Rishikesh, India
www.inner-light-in.com

First published 2010
Reprinted 2013

E-mail: innerlight.in@gmail.com

ISBN: 9788191026900

Disclaimer: The theory and the practices discussed in this book are for general information only. If you have recently experienced mental or emotional problems or are taking medication, you should seek professional medical advice or expert guidance before practicing meditation on your own. The authors and the publisher accept no responsibility for any harm caused by or to anyone as a result of misuse of these practices.

Dedication

We lovingly dedicate this book to the Inner Guru residing within you as pure love, light and blessedness, as your truest and deepest Self.

Contents

INTRODUCTION

Inner Guru is an eternal power, a principle that resides within your very being. We were connected to this infinite power from our very birth. When we grew up, we lost the connection, somehow, as we were cocooned in our forgetfulness, in our habitual pattern of obsessive thoughts, false beliefs and strong veil of individuality. Awakening the inner Guru could mean awakening the infinite potential of all good and all auspiciousness within us.

We can be awakened to it now, by being conscious of it and by being more receptive and open to it. This power within us is that part of us, which allows us to experience emotional mastery, keeps us calm, gives us the right guidance, and makes us happy and confident. It makes us able to attract to ourselves all good things of life.

This era has seen massive expansion of consciousness. We are living at an age when not only old and devoted spiritual practitioners, but even young and dynamic people from almost every walk of life are searching for the meaning and secret of Life. More and more people are being attracted to yoga and spirituality.

Yet, most people do not know what they are looking for, in their search. Why it is that so many seekers involved in the spiritual quest usually accomplish very little, not to speak of reaching the zenith of spiritual realization, even after years of sincere effort? The reason is obvious. If you do not know what you are searching in the name of spirituality, it will remain beyond your reach. If you search for anything outside your being, it will go on eluding you.

Do you know what it is really that you are searching for, in the name of spirituality? Is it the vision of an entity called God or Brahman? Is it a state of experience called, Nirvana or Samadhi? Or else, is it some supernatural powers? It absolutely depends upon you, what you really want. However, knowing where you want to go helps you reach the destination in a definite way. In reality, though, all searches are unconscious searches for bliss and peace, which is our real inner essence. This essence is our inner Guru, our being of limitless bliss.

Many questions arise, which almost every intelligent seeker has to confront on the path, at a certain point of time. What is the purpose of this existence? What do the words such as God, Self or Brahman, Buddha nature or Christ consciousness mean? Do all of them point to the same reality? Most importantly, does such a reality exist at all? The ancient scriptures and prophets tell us that it exists. Is it true or, is it some fabricated imagination of some fertile brains? If it really exists, why peace and fulfilment seems to remain just beyond the reach of majority of the seekers in spite of their frantic search? Is loyalty to a human Guru must for the spiritual evolution of a seeker? The answers available in the traditional books of spirituality do not seem to satisfy always. One has to look within.

An inquisitive mind is a sure sign of intelligence, nevertheless. While you need to have a humble and receptive mind to benefit from the prudence of our predecessors, you should regard with caution anything that asks you of blind obedience and following. You need to follow the path with the spirit of a scientist, with a mind unclouded with prejudices, neither accepting nor rejecting, but trying everything to see it for yourself. Belief and surrender to anything outside of your inner being brings slavery and bondage. Surrender to your inner power liberates you.

As you embark on the journey on this path, you will find that there is no well-defined route. It is a journey more like the flight of the swans that leave no trace behind when they fly. Still, there are pointers and landmarks, which, if known in the beginning, could be of immense help. In this book, we tried to give a systematic and thorough understanding of the path. We have discussed methods and techniques that will help you to awaken the inner light, the real guru existing within you. Unless the inner Guru is awakened, all searches outside would be futile, leaving you almost the same as when you started the search.

The term Guru has several connotations. It is widely used nowadays. Any teacher, in any field of expertise is called a Guru, for example, an information technology Guru, a management Guru or a music Guru. This type of usage of the word is okay, considering the indispensable necessity of having reverence and gratitude towards anybody from whom you learn something of worth.

However, in the ancient times, the word Guru referred only to the perfected master or the spiritual preceptor who guided the seeker to the ultimate truth of existence. Time has changed and, with it, changed the connotation of the word. In the modern era, it is not only difficult to find an able personal guidance in the field of spirituality to guide the seeker to the ultimate Truth; it is also difficult for the individual seeker to abandon all the responsibilities of family and society to sit at the feet of a Guru in the pursuit of Truth.

The term guru used in this book has quite a different meaning from its usual ancient as well as modern connotation. The inner Guru is a power, a principle that resides within you. This is a principle that resides in your very being, waiting to find expression to make your life a continuous song of fulfilment. It exists within you, beneath your thoughts, like a clear stream hidden under the sands, stones and pebbles. It is a repository of infinite strength, wisdom, abundance and auspiciousness. It is neither male, nor female. It is never a human being; yet, it is very much human as our most intimate and loveable friend that is ever eager to guide us to the life of glory and fulfilment, here and hereafter. It is the very essence of our inner being.

Most people are asleep to this fact. Most people remains closed off from this intimate source of auspiciousness existing at the core of their being. Unless you awaken to this power, it will be dormant, remaining only as a remote possibility, never actualising in your life as the glory and fulfilment you are destined to, the very moment you were born.

We are here on the earth for living a life of wisdom, love, joy and celebration. However, very few of us really believe and acknowledge the fact that life should never be a boring drudgery to carry on. Unfortunately, boredom, drudgery and un-fulfilment have become accepted norms of life, while, the reality should be just the contrary. God has manifested as human being with unlimited potential and unbounded freedom of choice. Whatever situations we are in, is a result of conscious or unconscious choices made by us.

Awakening the inner Guru is an indispensable necessity of life, whether or not you have somebody whom you revere as your Guru. The same inner potential insufficiently manifests and may help you through the outer form of a Guru, when you are not ready to awaken your inner Guru. Outer form of Guru is often a very distant token of that infinitely loving and compassionate inner Guru that abides within you through all the ups and downs, all the peaks and valleys of your life.

No human being, however great, can make our life blessed with continuous fulfilment. Peace and fulfilment are inner states of our being. Nobody from outside can make them manifest in our consciousness. Only our inner Guru can lovingly lead us to the supremely blissful summit of human existence, as we wake up to this reality.

Awakening is the ultimate of religion. Religion is, not really, in believing something outside of your being. It is not in believing or following some authoritative figure, the church, temple, organization or any ideological system of belief. Religion is trusting in what is eternal within you, your inner light, the Guru within. It is trusting in yourself, in the divinity within you that remains masked in the human body known as yourself.

With this trust, the inner Guru will be awakened to reveal the real you, as a grace, a beauty and splendour unknown to you so far. If that really happens to you, a deep inner silence, joy and peace will fill your being. You will find that, the life your mind had so long woven around you, with its hopes and frustrations, fears and anxieties, likes and dislikes, fleeting joys and sorrows, is not as real as you usually think of them. It is not as real as your real being of unlimited grace is. Your real being is a being, filled with blessedness that does not contain a trace of a shadow within it. As you wake up to this truth of your being, you will artlessly radiate a silent love that is not an emotion but a blessedness expressing itself as a tender benevolence towards all the existence. You will be a blessing to the existence.

The purpose of this book is not to preach a doctrine or provide you with a new set of belief to hold on to. This book is to help you to wake up to an existential reality that is already within you.

We lovingly offer this book to you, our worthy readers, in the hope that it will be a companion to your search for meaning of Life, Truth, God or blessedness. We believe that this book will find its way to those who are ready for a radical inner transformation. Read this book slowly, may be, one page or one section at a time. Assimilate the subject deeply within, and then put it in to practice. May all peace and blessedness be yours; it surely will be, as your inner Guru becomes your guide.

Chapter One

KNOWING THE NATURE OF INNER GURU

"Be the Light that you are.
Take refuge in your inner light."
- The Buddha

In the sacred shrine of your heart, there is an amazing light burning ceaselessly. This eternal light is the subtle principle that resides within all of us, which is unborn and undying. It is a repository of infinite strength, wisdom, abundance and auspiciousness. It is bliss infinite and the giver of supreme happiness. It is the support-less, infinite sky of supreme wisdom. It is the silent witness of everything. It is neither male, nor female. It exists beyond all dualities. It is never bounded by time, space or conditions. This witnessing presence is pure and clear like the sky, luminous like the morning Sun. It is our inner Guru.

It is beyond imagination and free from the natural forces of modification. It is revealed as the pure awareness of being. It is the witnessing silence beyond the blissful sheath, known as the 'I am', the pure thought of being. It was there before you were born; it will be there with you, when you drop your physical body to pass in to another plane of existence; or else, if all your earthly desires are exhausted, you may merge with it as your cosmic Self.

It is the eternal friend, philosopher and guide that always abides by you, no matter what external situation of life you might be going through. It never deserts you at any circumstances. It never deserts you however fallen you might be, judging your external state of being. It is the destroyer of all fears. It is the force, which ends the wheel of birth and death. It is our real Guru.

The Inner Sun

The word Guru, in Sanskrit, means that which removes or dispels darkness. 'Gu' in Sanskrit means darkness and 'Ru' is synonymous to light. The word 'guru' literally means the light that dispels darkness. Darkness exists inside all sentient beings in the form of ignorance of their real nature. Anger, hatred, fear, greed, jealousy, infatuation and the like, are offshoots of ignorance. They cloud the light of consciousness to make a person miserable.

All misery is darkness. In fact, darkness does not have any real substantial existence. It is not something tangible that you can get hold of and remove. You have to bring the light in order to remove the darkness. Darkness comes from nowhere, in the absence of light, and it just disappears in to nothing as soon as the light is there. Guru means the light that removes darkness from our heart, from our lives.

This light is our inner Sun. This inner Sun is our sole refuge, our protection. It is our supreme benefactor. We live by this light; we breathe by it and have our beings within it. It is inside as well as outside of our beings. We are nourished and sustained by it. It is a light that exists in all but belongs to none. All the beings and things belong to it. Your inner Guru already exists within you, shrouded in the veil of your ignorance and forgetfulness. When you are blissful and filled with gratitude, you are unknowingly connected to your inner Guru.

We, all of us, carry this eternal light in our hearts, within our inner being. However, ironically, being completely oblivious of this light, most of us search for it outside, in the external objects. All desires, material as well as spiritual, are, really, unconscious prayers. They are prayers for moving from darkness to light, from temporal to eternal, from death to immortality, from misery to happiness.

Ironically, we can not find permanent happiness and fulfilment in anything that exists outside of us. Things wear out, grow old, or loose their charm for us. This is the nature of all things and beings in this temporal plane of existence. Therefore, our search for light continues life after life, until one day we find the light within our inner being. When you trust the Guru within, you become open and receptive to the healing potential lying within the depth of your being. You become available to the light to remove all the darkness.

Our Real Self

The nature of the inner Guru is the nature of our true Self. It is the supreme in-dweller of all sentient and insentient beings. It is the eternal and changeless substratum of the whole existence. It is more intimate to us than our own breath. It is more intimate to us than our own heart, liver, or the marrow within our bone. It is the essence of our inner self. It is our deeper Self, our unlimited Self. It is that part of us, which allows us to experience emotional mastery, keeps us calm, gives the right guidance, and makes us happy and confident.

It is the infinitely loving and protecting core of our inner being. Infinite bliss is its essence. Its true nature can not be expressed in words. It is to be realized through the language of silence. It is the very source of all purity. Thinking about its nature makes us pure. Contemplating its nature makes us perfect. Meditating on its nature reminds us of our real nature as the limitless, boundless being. It is the ancient law of being, the unquestionable law behind the entire universe.

The Transcendental Power

This mystical power of the Guru within you can transform your life by bringing you all the happiness, peace and freedom, if you trust and rely on it. This power lies dormant within you until when you learn about it and begin to invoke this mystical power to find your true place in life. This is the power of all pervading pure consciousness. The power of your Inner Guru is beyond all measures. This power directs all the vital processes and functions of your body. It directs the functioning of your heart, the circulation of your blood, digestion and assimilation of food that you take in. It also guides the movement of the stars in the distant galaxies. It is the common ground of the whole existence. It knows the answers to all problems. It never sleeps. It is cosmic, and it is independent of time and space.

This wonderful power of your inner Guru can make you free from all bondages, earthly and spiritual, when you believe in it as your real self and access its power. This power governs the billions of cells in your body to act in precision, in an integrated manner.

Remember this power, stay connected to this power and let it flow through your Life. Then wonders will happen in your life. It is the power of your infinite, limitless being. To be aware of this power and to manifest it in every aspect of your life is your divine birthright. This power is the presence of God within you.

The Supreme Benefactor

Our inner Guru is the fulfiller of all the healthy desires. It is the remover of all unhealthy desires. It is the remover of all negative forces from our lives. It is the destroyer of all darkness of negative thoughts within and inauspicious situations outside. It is the supreme benefactor, which provides us with all good things of life. It manifests as the vital force of the living beings. It is the remover of all obstacles from our lives. This supreme guiding force pervades everything in this existence.

Most people block them off from this innate source of blessedness that exists at the core of their being. This power stays dormant within us until we wake up to acknowledge its presence.

The God-Essence within Us

The light of the inner Guru shines in the heart of all beings. The whole of plant and animal kingdom is evolving through this power, on an unconscious level. Only the human beings, intelligent as we are, have the miraculous capacity to be conscious of this hidden treasure, thereby accelerating our growth on the scale of evolution. We have the capacity to manifest the seed of God-essence, hidden within, to make the life a saga of joy and fulfilment.

On the other hand, only the human beings have the capacity to block this light through creating a veil of constant thinking, false beliefs and ego driven attitudes, thereby retarding their growth on the scale of evolution. We, all of us, are inherently destined to manifest as the godly beings that is waiting as a seed within us.

The Healing Light of Love

Our inner Guru is of the nature of formless light of cosmic oneness that illumines all our experiences. This light exists in the core of our being and permeates every cell of our body. It exists as a field of unconditional love. It is a love that never withers away. It knows all and holds all, saints and sinners alike, in its loving embrace of perfect understanding. It is a love that knows no division, no segregation, no darkness and no rejection. It is the common substratum, which supports, sustains and nourishes all the beings. It sees no fault of us because clear and penetrating is its vision. This light of pure love heals us and makes us whole.

We are not strangers in this journey of life on this planet. We are connected to each other through this mysterious field of love. This is the ground of our existence and we share it with all the creatures, whether the egoistic mind recognizes it, or not. This pure Love is of the nature of fullness where non-being manifests as being and being passes in to non-being. It is that awesome void where every form is born and dissolved in to the embrace of nothingness. It is that pure silence where every sound is born and hushed in to soundlessness. It is the stillness where every self is created and uncreated. It is peace throbbed with the melodies of Life. It is the state of ultimate glory of being.

It is detached, self-assured, self-poised, non-possessive and non-aggressive in nature. Yet, it is tremendously powerful to move the whole universe. The whole universe is actually moving by the power of this love. It saturates and permeates every fibre of this existence. Its mere presence directs the change of seasons, the flow of the rivers and movement of all beings.

This omnipresent love exists within us as our inner being. Everything that is alive is a wonderful, expression of this love. It manifests itself as the breath moving in all living beings. It shines as this moment here and now. It is the Life eternal expressing itself as this ephemeral, transient and momentary existence.

It shines as a serene understanding of the underlying oneness of all beings. This love is not an emotion; nor is it a virtue. It is a necessity that is the very sap of life. This ancient, ever-present and unborn love is that presence what makes any earthly love an unfailing source of bliss and fulfilment. Yet, the earthly love, most often marred by lust, jealousy and possessiveness, is but a poor reflection of this magnificent light.

The love of a man for a woman or vice versa is but a distant token of this splendour that this primordial Love is. The love of a mother for her child is but a threshold to the holy temple where this Glory resides. Real nature of this Love is love for the all-embracing Self. It is a presence, which holds everything in the weave of oneness. It needs no one to exalt it. This Love exalts the heart that it finds worthy of itself.

It exists in all creatures and human beings, though in most places it is covered with unawareness, doubt or distrust. Most of us spend the whole life asleep to this light. In the cocoon of the forgetfulness of our Inner light, we weave dreams of fear, struggle, conflict and negative emotions that beset the earthly existence and make the life seem like a burden.

This inner light within us has the power to heal every situation of life. The inner Guru is always there shining with the splendour of a thousand Suns to dispel the darkness of all false identifications and negativities to reveal and illumine our true nature as unconditional love. This happens when we open the doors of our hearts, when we make ourselves receptive and ready to dissolve in to the grace. Only then, this ever-present light of unconditional love shines in the heart to guide us through this journey of life to peace and fulfilment.

Life is an Opportunity

Love is the light and bliss is its radiance. All sentient beings carry this light of love within them, though unaware of it. The human beings are endowed with a nervous system so wonderful and sophisticated that we are capable of being aware of this light and by being aware of this light, we become the light, which illumines our earthly being.

Yet, so few are there who try to actualize this potential hidden within them. Most people waste the opportunity. Most people squander away this precious gift of life in pursuit of trinkets of tinsels in the world external to them. Human life is very precious. Do not waste it. Do not waste your time searching for a teacher or a technique. If someone says that, it will take many births for you to get liberation, never believe. If someone says that God, Nirvana or salvation is far away from you, never believe. If you are taught that your salvation depends on your allegiance to some external figure or organization, then be on guard. It is far from truth. Whatever may be your past, if you are sincere, one lifetime is sufficient to get liberation, or realization of your true nature. It waits within you to be discovered, welcomed and embraced by you.

Trust and rely on your Inner Guru to guide you. If you do not find your inner Guru, you will always have to look outside for the answers. These answers will help you to some extent, but until you fully empower yourself by connecting to your inner Guru, you will never experience peace and satisfaction at a deep and sustainable level. Unless you discover and realize the inner light, your human life will remain unfulfilled, a huge potential underutilised and wasted. This human life is a great opportunity. It is an opportunity to uncover our being of light. All of us are entitled to have the blessing of living an enlightened life, a life lighted with love, peace, joy and freedom.

Chapter Two

INNER GURU AND OUTER GURU

"The light of the body is the eye: if therefore your eye be single, your whole body shall be full of light."
- Matthew 6:22

Have you ever thought what is it that sees through your eyes? Eyes are made of flesh and blood, which are inert objects themselves. When the apparatus called eye does not function properly, it can be operated upon or replaced by artificial lenses. So, eyes can not see. It is something else that sees through the eyes. What is it? Eyes are called the light of the body. What is it that is the light of your eyes? It is you, the conscious principle behind the eyes, which sees through the eyes.

Although our true nature is pure consciousness, this real nature of us is often obscured by the dark cloud of ignorance and delusion. Our human play is staged by the self-hypnotized, self-limiting aspect of the consciousness. In a human form, the consciousness has two aspects. In one aspect, consciousness is playing the drama of human life in forgetfulness of its true nature; while in another aspect, consciousness remains pure, shining, blissful and conscious of its one, indivisible and infinite nature. This aspect of consciousness, hidden deep within us, is our inner Guru. In its infinite compassion, this inner Guru works tirelessly for our evolution. It works life after life, until we break away from the illusion of smallness to return to the glory and spaciousness of our real being.

The inner Guru often manifests in the form of an outer teacher. In its external manifestation, the inner Guru can appear in any form whatsoever. It appears to help us, to illumine our intellect so that we gradually learn to grasp the ultimate essence. Sometimes it may appear as a person and sometimes as an insentient thing. It can manifest as human or animal, as wind or rain, as mountain or ocean, and, even as a grain of sand that may suddenly illumine your intellect to flood you with insights. A pot, a jar, an ordinary wooden cot in your room, even a mossy wall in your courtyard may be transform itself to the luminous manifestation of consciousness to teach you the law of omnipresence. When this power is awakened, you will find its sermon in the soil in your garden, in the rays of the morning Sun, in the eyes of another human being, or even in the eyes of a dog.

Life: the Greatest Teacher

Life is a journey, a school where we learn from people, things and experiences, as we move along. Anything and everything can be a teacher to us, if we are open and receptive to learn. All the people we interact with, all our sorrow and happiness have something to teach us, to lead us towards the highest rung of evolution.

At different phases of life, we have to come across different teachers, from whom we learn things to enhance our lives. Our learning started when we were born and it continues as we grow. The willingness to learn is a great virtue. It helps us evolve faster than anything does. Learning something new makes our brain cells grow, keeping us young. Learning is the way of life.

Whosoever helps us to learn something of worth may be called as the guru. However, in the spiritual sense of the term, Guru is the teacher, a master, whom you can trust, who guides you in your thoughts and actions to lead you further in your evolution. When a child is born, it learns to speak and walk, knows things and persons with the help of its mother. Hence, mother is often referred as the first guru. Then, we learn things from our teachers in the schools and colleges, from our friends, from various books. We learn from the teachings of the spiritual masters, who point to us a higher purpose of our existence. Everywhere in life, you have the scope to learn the lessons in abundance, only if you are ready. Life itself is the greatest of all teachers.

Role of Outer Gurus

Although our greatest teacher, the real teacher is our inner Guru, initially, some may need external help in order to awaken the inner Guru. Receiving the help with honour, gratitude and dignity will help us to grow. As we receive the teachings with a grateful heart, with love and respect to the teachers that come into our lives, our inner potentials open up. Outer guru is none other than the embodiment and representative of the inner Guru. It is said that when you are ready, guru will come to you automatically.

The teacher-student relationship can be extremely beneficial to one's personal growth and the benefit can not be understated. There are instances where surrender to an external form of the guru helped a seeker to reach the highest evolution of consciousness. An able teacher works as a lamp to ignite your inner essence. Energy is transmitted from the guru to the disciple to provide the necessary ignition. However, it is very difficult to find such an able personal guidance nowadays. If you are fortunate enough to have a master whose human form and wisdom, you come to love deeply, know that, this human form is none other than the external manifestation of the mystery of your inner truth. This will help you evolve faster.

Nevertheless, being too much attached to the physical form of the guru not only binds one in the bodily plane of existence, it also obstructs the flow of inner light. Sometimes, the ego-boosting attitude of glorifying one's own guru binds the seeker in a subtle way. Moreover, having an outer guru often becomes a good excuse to avoid the inner journey. Many people think that, taking the mantra initiation from a guru is enough; from then on, the guru would take care of all their karma as well as their spiritual growth. This is a misconception. One has to take responsibility of his own life. You have to walk the path yourself. Nobody can realize for you what you want to realize.

Nature as the Guru

Not always, gurus come in the human form. As we have already said, sometimes a tree, a bird, a book, or even a stone can teach you a profound lesson. If you are tuned, receptive and alert, you will get the right direction and right message at the right time from many sources of Nature. Many of our ancient sages took the Sun, the Sky or the Fire as their guru.

In Upanishad, we have the story of sage Yajnavalkya who worshipped the Sun as his guru and obtained knowledge. Yajnavalkya was a disciple of Vaishampayana. Once he apparently had a debate with his guru. His guru got angry with him as the latter is said to display too much pride in being abler than other students. Yajnavalkya was asked by his guru to return whatever he had learnt from him. Yajnavalkya immediately quits and determines not to have any human guru thereafter.

He accepted the Sun as his guru because the Sun abides in all beings as the supreme Self as its rays surround all beings like the sky. He prayed to the Sun for acquiring the fresh Vedic knowledge that his preceptor Vaishampayana did not know. In doing so, what he did, albeit unknowingly, was turning to his inner Guru, the inner light that is one, indivisible and not restricted by limiting conditions. Yajnavalkya received the new wisdom, from the Sun. It is said that the Sun god took the form of a horse and graced the sage with the wisdom that was not known to others. This portion of the Vedic knowledge revealed to Yajnavalkya goes by the name of Shukla Yajurveda.

In the Upanishads, we have many such stories where the guru appeared in forms other than that of a human being. We have the fascinating story of the sage Satyakam

Jabala. The boy and his poor mother Jabala were living at the end of a forest. Satyakam grew up a promising boy. He was truthful, fearless, sincere, and aflame with a thirst for knowledge. As Satyakam grew up, he knew that he was born of a poor courtesan woman. Consequently, he did not have a family name, and could not know who his father was.

However, this staggering fact could not abate Satyakam's thirst for knowledge. He went to the guru Goutama, desiring the knowledge of Brahman. Goutama, the acclaimed teacher of that day, accepted him, but, did not teach him directly. Instead, he ordered Satyakam to go to the forest and take care of thousands of sick and weak cows, until they were doubled in number. Service to the guru was regarded with highest respect in those days. Satyakam followed the instruction of his guru. In his forest dwelling, he lived alone, tending the cows, and forgot everything about the world outside. In course of time, when the cows were doubled in number, he was not even aware of that. He spent his time in the solitude of the forest, absorbed within himself, accomplishing his duty. Ultimately, he was blessed with the great wisdom, which came to him in a strange way, from unexpected sources. A Bull, a Swan, a little Cormorant and the Fire taught him the supreme knowledge of Brahman. This story is symbolic of the fact that, neither the association of a human guru nor the study of scripture is essential to be awakened to the ultimate Truth. Knowledge comes automatically, when you are ready, when the inner flower blossoms.

Art of Discipleship

Life itself becomes the guru to one, rich in the art of discipleship. We have the story of the enlightened sage Avadhut Dattatreya who had acknowledged the help from as many as twenty-four gurus in his life. An Avadhut is one who had cut asunder the bondage of ignorance to live in the bliss of his Self. Dattarreya's relationship with each of his gurus did not consist of didactic lectures or intellectual discussions. Dattatreya had accepted the Earth, the air, the sky, the water, the fire, the moon, the Sun, a child, and even a courtesan woman as his guru, as he wondered along the path of his life.

To Dattatreya, discipleship meant receptivity and flexibility of the mind. It was the capacity to see with an open mind, to see beyond the forms into the essence of things. He discarded all the mind-made concepts, notions or intellectual explanations. He had a state of consciousness that was fired with an intense longing to experience the truth as it is. His was a spirit that learns from all of existence with the innocence of a child.

With this wonderful spirit of discipleship, Dattatreya responded to the entire world around him. This wonderful faculty of discipleship endowed him with the capacity to renounce concept after concept, experience after experience, in order to reach the inner sanctuary of truth.

Accepting Multiple Teachers

It is immaterial, whether you have one guru or many. Guru in any form actually represents a principle that is beyond human intellect, beyond the space-time trajectory. Many of the sages had more than one guru. The divine always blesses us from many directions and through many channels. Life has many ways, multiple avenues to lead us towards higher evolution. In this search for truth, one needs to be receptive. If you keep yourself closed to a single channel, your evolution may be retarded.

However, people often forget that, in reality, Guru is a supreme principle that a person may represent. As a result, over the time the guru had become an institution or a cult that demanded unflinching loyalty from the disciples. Many superstitions were born that barred people to go elsewhere for knowledge, once they accepted someone as the guru. It is of paramount importance to acknowledge and respect anybody you might have benefited from. Nevertheless, it should be in the freedom of the individual to go and search for knowledge elsewhere, if the existing help is not adequate. If someone is not happy with his external guru, he should have the freedom to leave with all humbleness and search elsewhere. When one door is closed, many other doors open, by the grace of the inner Guru.

The relation between the outer guru and the disciple should not be that of a master and a slave. It should not be a relation creating the bondage of perpetual slavery. Narrow sectarianism, religious blindness, dogmatism, intolerance of other faiths and sects, and many other evils are born from this wrong notion, which further bind a seeker instead of liberating him. Mutual love and respect should form the bonding between a guru and disciple, which does not restrict a seeker in his search for knowledge.

Gautama the Buddha had many gurus. After abandoning his kingdom, he moved from one teacher to another, in his quest for the way of cessation of sorrow. In his search for the truth, he travelled the length and breadth of India learning from many teachers. He greatly benefited from his teachers Alara Kalama and Rudraka Ramaputra who showed him the way to reach and abide in deep meditative consciousness. However, his thirst for truth remained unabated, as he did not find the answer to his question. Nobody could show him the way to go beyond sorrow. Ultimately, he abandoned all, to rely solely on his inner wisdom and attained nirvana, the ultimate inner awakening to truth. He discovered the noble eightfold path as the way to complete cessation of sorrow.

In this context, it should be clear that, once you accept someone as your guru, you must have trust on that person and practice with faith and respect. Once you have allegiance to a form of practice, you must put your heart and soul in to it. In addition, you must be sincere to give it enough time to test whether it is working for you. You must persevere in spiritual practices with an earnest, open and receptive heart. Your search for truth must be genuine. Otherwise, one may endlessly move from one human guru to another expecting to learn something new, but never seeing the light of truth. Nobody can give you the experience of truth, unless you are ready. The flower of truth is an inner subjective experience that blossoms in the right season, when the soil of mind is ready through earnest practices and the seed of inner quest has sprouted in to the tree of inner wisdom.

Death as Guru

Death is an experience that no mortal can avoid. It comes to people, unexpected and unwanted. People are afraid even to talk about this inevitable phenomenon of their lives. This is because people have associated death with pain, the pain of the decaying body, pain of departing from the near and dear ones, pain of falling in to the unknown. Nobody wants pain. Hence, even the word 'death' is surrounded by fears. There is the fear of uncertainty, fear of letting go of all the accumulations and possessions of this life. Nevertheless, death can be the most prolific teacher in life, if we can remain alert and aware at the time of death. In the life of sage Raman Maharshi, intense fear of death served as the guru that led him to the experience of his deathless Self. He found that death could not take his eternal being away from him. In Upanishad, we have the story of Nachiketa, whom the lord of death himself instructed in the knowledge of the Self. The Lord of death, as the guru, taught him the secret of life and death.

We have the story of the enlightened king Janaka that reminds us of the powerful practice of contemplating on one's own death while engaging in all the affairs of life. In spite of leading the life of a householder, Janaka was a sage and seer of extraordinary wisdom. People regarded him as a *Jivanmukta*, the one who attained liberation while living in this very body. Once, a young spiritual seeker was sent to Janaka by his preceptor. Desiring spiritual teachings, this young aspirant came to the court of Janaka, walking through many villages and many forests. Nevertheless, the disappointment of this young man knew no limits when he found the king Janaka surrounded by the luxuries of the royal life, with beautiful dancers dancing in his court and the king Janaka himself dressed in splendid royal robes and ornaments. Fragrances and songs were in the air and Janaka with all his ministers were apparently enjoying all these pomp and luxury. The young seeker was flabbergasted. He was thinking, what a *Brahmacharin*, a celibate and ascetic like him could possibly learn from a king like this, who was immersed in such splendour of materialism.

Janaka noticed the boy just when he was about to leave the court silently. He summoned the boy and on enquiring about his purpose for coming to him, he requested the boy to stay for the night and leave in the morning. The boy relented to his request, hiding his dismay. After feeding him with a sumptuous meal in the night, Janaka arranged for the boy to stay in one of the most beautiful rooms of the palace. However, when the boy rested his tired body on the soft, white bed, he discovered in his terror that all over the ceilings of the room there were sharp swords hanging down, tied in very fine threads. Any moment the slightest breeze could move the swords and any one of them could fall down to pierce his chest, or sever his head. The door of the room was locked from outside. The boy could not close the lids of his eyes in the night and waited for the daybreak in constant terror, looking at the swords.

In the morning, King Janaka himself opened the door smilingly, enquiring about his well-being. Tired and enraged after the ordeal of the night, the boy shot back with a sharp answer. What kind of hospitality this was! He asked how the king could expect anyone to rest, much less to have a good sleep in such a room where swords were hanging over the head everywhere. Janaka smiled, begged apologies from the boy and said; he arranged this to explain something that the boy possibly came to learn. He said, "My boy, just as you could not enjoy the luxurious bed with swords hanging above, I too can never be engrossed in the luxuries around me, since, I continuously remember the impermanence of life. It is, as if, the sword of death is hanging above my head and it may fall on me any moment. This unseen sword is hanging on everybody. Remember death and impermanence of everything. Remember it continuously, contemplate over it and you will be on the right track always. Ultimately, you will find the truth." The boy received the teaching, learnt the secret of greatness of Janaka and left with a glad heart. Death can serve as the guru when one patiently contemplates on it, while alive.

Though this narrative may be metaphorical and seems extreme to some extent, we have a lesson to learn from it. You never really know in which form the inner Guru appears in its external manifestation to teach you. Receptivity, openness and fearlessness makes one prepared to enter the palace of wisdom.

The process called 'Death' can give us the glimpse of our immortal nature, if we are ready. Death can serve us as the Guru, to give us the knowledge of our deathless Self, while it takes away all that is unnecessary and external to our real being. Death can lead us to the presence of a wonderful Love, which our inner Guru is, if we learn to trust it, instead of being afraid.

In Tibet, practices are in vogue among the Buddhist monks that teach them to face death with courage and peace, with their awareness calm and centred within. The Buddha himself taught the meditation on death. It makes us fearless, peaceful and mindful of the impermanence of life.

Guru Kripa

Guru Kripa literally means the grace of guru, which is essential for the spiritual evolution. Grace comes from your inner shrine when you are sincere, open and receptive. Grace comes when you trust. Trusting your inner Guru is actually, trusting your very own self. It is that part of yourself, which does not appear on the surface, but stays deep under your subconscious mind, as the silence, which exists on the background of your 'I am'. Unless you trust that there is something behind your surface personality, that is all powerful and very essence of you, you will not be able to access the grace of your inner Guru when you need. The light of grace is always flowing and it can transform you, only if you allow yourself to flow with it. The inner Guru is the essence of your being. When you surrender to it, your false dream of smallness vanishes and your life is blessed.

Reverence to Sat-Guru

It is said that reverence and surrender to the sat-guru are the key to open the knots of life. Who is a sat-guru? '*Sat*' means real; sat means that which abides eternally. It means the eternal backdrop on which the multiple names and forms appear and disappear in course of time, like illusory images. 'Guru' is the illumining principle, the witnessing energy of consciousness, which removes the darkness or ignorance. What is ignorance? Ignorance is a notion or belief that makes us identify with a form, any form, with the help of thoughts such as "I am this form", or "This form is mine"; while in reality, we are formless energy of consciousness. This identification with forms, which are all ephemeral, makes us suffer.

The word 'sat-guru' literally means the illuminating presence that abides eternally to remove the darkness of ignorance. Evidently, it can never be a human being because no human form can abide eternally. The term automatically refers to the inner illumining principle, the inner Guru.

Nevertheless, in conventional usage of the term, sat-guru refers to a teacher who has realized this 'sat' as his inner essence; who has realized the inner Guru, as his real self. Consequently, he can help you too, to realize the inner Guru as your real Self. The outer form of a guru is actually a channel through which the inner power expresses itself. Nevertheless, any teacher, whoever might have helped you on the path, is worthy of your respect and gratitude. When you receive a sublime teaching that transforms your life, respect and gratitude would surge in your heart as a spontaneous flowering. That itself is the worship of the inner Guru. True love and devotion can transform your narrow human existence in to the spacious expansion of consciousness that encompasses all. True devotion can work as a wonderful alchemy that can change all the mundane things in to the sacred and divine. When the mind is imbued with devotion to your own inner Self, all your thoughts and actions are liberated in the subtle presence of the guru as humble offerings of fragrant flowers of multiple colours. This is the meaning of true worship.

A real guru knows that the inner Guru is your ultimate guide and makes you aware of that presence within you. Rare is such a teacher, and rarer is a disciple who is prepared to receive and assimilate such a teaching. When you love, respect or worship such a teacher, the worship actually goes to the inner Guru that manifests as the teacher and as the teachings. Unfortunately, nowadays, this noble emotion of reverence to sat-guru has often been reduced to formal ritualistic observance and blind organizational obedience. In most places, this amounts to mental slavery and bondage, which becomes the breeding ground for narrow sectarianism. Real love never binds you; it makes you free. True love and devotion kindles your own inner light. Real devotion is not mindless and undiscriminating following of another's whims or personality; it is not dumping your karma on your guru, relinquishing your own responsibility towards yourself; it is not standing in the long queue hoping to have a glimpse of your guru or offering some flowers showing your respect.

Real devotion is an unbroken longing for the truth, which manifests itself as silent reverential gratitude. Real love is a humble receptivity of a silent heart that is prepared to melt and merge in the divine. While love and devotion to your teacher helps you to grow, if you are able to see your teacher not as a human being, but as an expression of your own inner light, that would be the source of the highest blessing. That inner light, the inner Guru is your greatest teacher.

Always feel connected to that inner light, and not to the mere physical form of the external guru. Attachment to the external form of a guru sometimes creates bondage. This is why Buddha said, "Rely on the message of the teacher, not on his personality; rely on the meaning of his words, not on the words." This is extremely important to remember.

The Inner Voice

If you are sincere in your search there comes a time when you simply outgrow the need for a human guru. In the presence of a guru, you can learn the art of merging in the infinite sky of your inner being. Then, there comes a point in your life when you no longer need an external guru. Attachment to the teacher-student relationship beyond this point can sometimes become a hindrance to one's growth. Even if you are fortunate to find an able guide in your life, a time comes when you have to move alone with your inner Guru. For your own growth, you need to drop the external supports. The real role of an outer guru is to teach us to receive the inner voice from our inner Guru and to make us realize the constant presence of this ultimate teacher within us. When you grow the ability to communicate with your higher Self, you find the Guru within you. The key to receiving inner guidance is to trust in yourself and to be open to the incredible and infinite possibility existing within you.

Prophet Mohammad learnt from his inner voice that directed him to read the Quran, though he was illiterate. The mysterious inner voice read through him, revealed to him the beautiful stanzas of the Quran. The Chinese mystic Lao Tzu also attuned himself with his inner silence to learn the mysteries of life from the Nature.

Listen to your own inner voice. Listen very attentively, very consciously, and you will never go wrong. When the inner Guru is awakened, the need for an outer Guru dissolves. When this awakening takes place, the disciple becomes one with the guru. You merge with your inner Guru. At the deepest and highest level of consciousness, the master and the disciple are not separate; they can not be separate in any way. Initially there was the difference between the teacher and the student; but, when the inner Guru is awakened, you merge with it as your own inner essence. The teacher and student become one, and the subject and object of study merge into a profound state of bliss. What is left, is Guru, the highest possible state of consciousness that manifests as the seeker and the sought, knower and the known, hunger and the food, thirst and the water, lover and the beloved, devotee and the God, part and the Whole.

Chapter Three

BODY, MIND AND INNER GURU

"Beyond the senses is the mind, beyond the mind is the intellect, higher than the intellect is the self, higher than the self is the Unmanifest (flow-energy of consciousness). Beyond the Unmanifest is the great indwelling Presence, the all-pervading (witness) and imperceptible. Having realized that, the embodied self becomes liberated and attains Immortality."

-*[Katha Upanishad 1:3:10-11]*

Know thyself to know the universe. This has been the decree of the Upanishads. From the ancient times, sages and seers entreat us to know ourselves. To know one is to know one's body, mind and soul. When we know ourselves to the deepest core of our being, we come to know the secret of this existence. This life is a song made of the musical rhythm of the body, words of the mind and the melodious silence of the soul. When the three are in harmony, the song becomes pure and pleasing to listen. If they are in disharmony, noises result and the song disappears. The inward journey to awaken the inner Guru will allow you to explore and integrate all the aspects of your being.

Body is a Part of the Nature

Our body is an incomparable creation of the Divine. It is a vehicle. The divine Self rides it to sport in this material plane of existence. As we begin our inner voyage, this body serves us as the boat. Our physical body is made of the elements from the nature, such as the earth, water, fire and air. There is space within and around the body on which these elements are woven to give a shape to the body. Consequently, our physical body is an extension of the Nature, '*Prakriti*', in Sanskrit.

The inputs we take from the Nature, as food, air, water or the fire element, directly affects our thoughts, emotions and the level of the vital energy in the body. Consequently, they affect the gross body as well as all the subtle bodies. We know how the nature of food affects the mind. This is very much evident when someone takes an intoxicating beverage or drugs. Certain drugs are capable of altering the state of consciousness. If the subtle bodies too were not part of the Nature as the gross body is, they were not affected by the external inputs. Therefore, all the layers of our subtle bodies are part of the Nature too. This human body is an integral part of this vast and magnificent existence.

Our Born Nature and the Unborn Nature

The Nature is in a constant flux, and so is the body. Body is a changing phenomenon. It is dying every moment to renew itself. However, there is definitely something, we intuitively understand, that does not change among the changing panorama of life. This is the reason why there is so much effort in this world to make permanent everything we value. This is the reason why we feel that we remain the same entity, though the body ages. Thus, the unconscious search for the absolute and unchanging reality within our being begins as insane efforts to keep up youthful appearance in an aging body.

Our ancients studied the body deeply to find out that our bodies are an indivisible part of Nature. Consequently, it follows the natural cycle of all natural things, viz., birth, growth, maturity, decay and destruction. Moreover, they found that all the work done by the body is actually done by the Nature. There is the inert nature and there is an intelligent nature within us. All the layers of the body belong to the inert nature, which is our born or manifested nature. We all have a born nature and an unborn or un-manifest nature.

The body is our born nature. Our born nature constitutes of this gross, physical body as well as all the subtle bodies like the mental body and the body of vital energy. The born nature is dying continuously, to transmute in to a newer one. All the actions of body and mind are done through this born nature. Energy of speech and action belongs to this born nature.

Just as our body and mind are our born nature, which is constantly changing, we have something within us that does not change. It is our unborn nature. Our unborn nature is the intelligent principle of pure being and knowing, that shines in every being as the 'I am'. It is really an indivisible part of the cosmic unborn nature, the Cosmic Self, which is the divine Self. Our unborn nature is our deathless self. It is made of pure energy of consciousness. This unborn nature is intelligent. It possesses the energy of volition and the energy of witnessing. When this unborn nature is fully realized as our real being, all the narrowness melts away and the fear of death vanishes as also to banish all other fears from our lives.

Even behind this unborn nature, the realm of self-aware Silence exists. It is our unborn essence. This self-aware presence is our real essence that lies beyond the Nature. All the idea of 'doing' belongs to Nature. Our real essence is pure being. Even the idea of the Self as the principle of pure being and knowing springs up from this essence and is supported by this essence. It is this essence, which shines as the witnessing silence, as the inner Guru, through the veil of the individual 'I am' as well as the Cosmic Self.

The Shrine of the Divine

In many parts of India, the ancient temples were built in a typical fashion. They have many layers. You have to cross many foyers, narrow and spacious, to have a glimpse of the deity in the innermost shrine of the temple. As we embark on the pilgrimage to enter the holy shrine of the divine within our body, we gradually move from the outermost layer towards the inner shrine.

In this inner journey, as we move from our physical body to our subtler bodies, we are surprised to find many layers of our being. We find that this physical body is just the outermost layer of a wonderful shrine, which consists of five layers.

We have an energy body, the seat of breath, vital energy and emotions. We have a mental body, the seat of thoughts and imaginations. We have an intellectual body, the seat of intelligence and wisdom; and then, we have the sheath of individuality, the blissful body as the subtlest part of our form. Even beyond our bliss body, there is our unborn essence that resides at the core of our being as the inner Guru. That divine core, though never absent from anyone, remains latent within us, waiting to be discovered.

Know your Energy Body

According to the yogic scriptures, we have subtle energy channels within the body known as Nadis. Nadi, in Sanskrit, means the energy channel or the energy river. Energy flows through these subtle channels of the body as water flows in the rivers. All our thoughts, emotions and physical states are expressions of the flow of vital energy along these energy channels. Therefore, energy body is the base for our constitution. It is the base for our physical body as well as the mind.

According to yogic scriptures, there are seventy-two thousands of nadis or subtle energy channels in the body. Among them, the nadis called Ida, Pingala and Sushumna are most important. They are also named after the rivers Ganga, Yamuna and Saraswati. The Ida begins from the right, and Pingala from the left near the coccyx of the body and both of them go up spirally crisscrossing one another forming energy centres in the process.

There are six main subtle nerve centres, called the chakras, or energy wheels. The first, situated at the base of the spine, is called the root chakra or the Muladhara chakra, meaning the wheel of basic support. The second is situated above it along the spine, at a point below the navel centre; it is called the Swadhisthana chakra, meaning the energy wheel that is the seat of the individual self. The third energy wheel is situated along the spine, at the back of the navel; it is called the Manipura chakra, meaning the energy vortex that houses a jewel within. The fourth energy wheel is formed along the spinal column at the back of the heart; it is called the Anahata chakra, meaning the wheel of the Unstruck sound. The fifth energy wheel exists along the spine at the base of the neck; it is called the Bishuddhi chakra, meaning the wheel that is purifying in nature. The sixth energy vortex is formed at the end of the spinal column, at the back of the centre of the eyebrows. The sixth chakra is called the Ajna chakra, meaning the wheel of command. The seventh is called the Sahasrara, meaning the wheel of a thousand streams. This seventh chakra lies beyond the physical body, above the crown. It is the wheel of transcendence. The individual energy flows out from this energy vortex to melt and merge with the cosmic Whole.

There are specific reasons for such names given to the energy centres, by the ancient yogis. For example,

Bishudhhi, in the Sanskrit means purifying. The Bishudhhi chakra or the energy vortex situated near the larynx is a wonderful purifier of energies and can transform toxic or disharmonious vibrations in to pure ones. Manipura, in Sanskrit, means the house of jewel. The Manipura chakra, at the navel is the seat of the precious jewel of life energy within the body.

When these energy wheels are clear of obstructions, the body and mind remains healthy and happy. If there are obstructions or distortions in the flow of energy radiated from any of the wheels, the body and mind becomes imbalanced, and diseases result. Wrong food and lifestyle, bad postures, stress, anxiety and other negative emotions block the energy channels. When energy can not flow freely along a channel, we experience it as a physical disease or mental distress. Flow is the nature of energy; flow is another name of life.

Sushumna, the Saraswati is the energy river that flows through the middle of these energy wheels rising straight to end in the Brahma Randhra, the area of the crown chakra. At the throat chakra, however, the Sushumna divides itself in to two, of which one rises through the back of the skull and the other through the front, along the bridge between the two nostrils, until they meet at the crown. So long as the mind flows to the external things and objects, left and right energy channels, that is, Ida and Pingala remains active. Sushumna, the central channel is almost blocked for most of the parts for majority of the people and needs to be cleared so that the vital energy may move through it. When the vital energy moves through the Sushumna, the body feels light and the mind becomes clear, tranquil and introvert.

Knowing the energy body is important for the understanding of our spiritual constitution. The energy body connects the gross physical sheath with all other sheaths. It is the energy body, which affects, and is affected by our thoughts, emotions and actions. Observation of our energy body through these external manifestations can lead us to many insights regarding the subtle layers of our being. The energy body bridges the body and the mind.

Mind: The Subtle Body

The mind is actually an extension of the body, the subtler part of it. It is more appropriate to say that the physical body is an extension of the mind. The mind is the subtle part of body as the body is the grosser part of mind. The mind is another manifestation of the same energy that makes the body. As a tree is rooted on the earth, the mind is rooted in this body.

The mind came in to existence as the consciousness, the pure being and knowing principle identified itself with the body. Because of this false identification, the thought, "I am the body", was born. This thought-entity is called the 'mind'. Your 'I' is made of pure energy of consciousness; it is the pure knowing and being principle. It can not be a form. It can not be a bodily being. Consciousness can never become one with a body. Hence, mind is a fictitious entity.

The body minus consciousness is an inert object having no capacity to function or survive. The same body, operating and alive a while before, becomes inert like a piece of wood, and is declared dead, as and when the consciousness leaves the body. This fact is known to all. Yet, we continue to think ourselves as the body and not as a conscious being. In essence, we are the energy of pure consciousness as the witness of our body, mind, intellect and surroundings.

Strangely, for a reason incomprehensible to ordinary human intellect, as we receive the vehicle of this body, we all forget our essential nature as consciousness embodied, and instead, begin to think ourselves as the body. Mind is the subtle body.

Mechanical Nature of Mind

The mind mostly behaves according to the programs stored within it, just as your computer operates according to the software programmed in to it. Our mind moves in habitual patterns along the known tracks that it is used to. Though the mind seems to be intelligent, it is no more intelligent than the modern supercomputer. Nevertheless, the mind started to behave as an intelligent entity by the power of pure consciousness. With little regards for our conscious permission, the mind goes on producing thoughts that float like clouds in the infinite sky of our consciousness. In a moment of excitement, fear, anxiety or anger, the thoughts and emotions become so dense that they completely cloud the inner sky of consciousness.

The mind not only creates thoughts and emotions, it also gathers them from the environment. It stores the habitual thought patterns, ideas and impressions as the memory, which it brings up from its reserve, in appropriate occasions. It also recycles the thoughts that were stored as the memory, and produces dreams during the hours of our sleep.

The deeper layer of the mind also has the capacity to discriminate between right and wrong, good or bad, and so on. It does so, according to the information provided by the data and knowledge stored in its reserve from the past instances. Any external or internal incident creates a sensation on the body, pleasant, painful or neutral; the mind saves the experience as a memory to be summoned for reference in the future. This past knowledge gives it the capacity to discriminate whether a particular thing or incident would be beneficial and joyful for the body, and it decides accordingly.

The mind was meant to be at our service and not to rule us as it normally does. Instead of using the mind, we are habituated to be used by the mind. The instrument designed for the survival of the body began to dictate its own terms and we lost the freedom that our true nature of perfect bliss is. The result is tension, sorrow and bondage. Only when we get a glimpse of our real nature as the eternal consciousness, we can regain our original kingdom of bliss.

Individual self, Personality and Real Self

What is the Self? Well, to be very precise, self is the idea: 'I am and I know'. At different levels of consciousness, the word has different connotations. Depending on the phase of one's life and the level of one's evolution, the word 'self' varies in its meaning. The meaning of this 'I' goes on changing at different phases of life, at different stages of evolution. When you were a child, your 'I' possibly represented a four year old boy or a girl having an innocent face which has little similarity with the image of the grown up face that you see in the mirror now. When you contemplate on this, you know that your body is just an image of the 'I', that you think yourself to be. The same is true for your mind, your thoughts, emotions and feelings. They are just changing images of your 'I', created around your bodily being.

The images go on changing. The real 'I' changes not. Therefore, your changing body and mind, at any particular point of space and time, is not your real 'I'. They are not your self. Though it seems so obvious, it is not so easy to get rid of the idea of the body as your self. When our consciousness abides in the peripheral existence of body and surroundings, the self seems to manifest as the body, mind and individuality.

The idea of individuality is a by-product of the growth of the mind. When the pure knowing and being consciousness erroneously identified itself with the body, it succumbed to the idea that its being was limited within the narrow confine of a body that is separate from the others, the other bodies. Thus, the idea of individuality was born. Just like the mind, the individual self is another idea, a fiction, to be more specific.

The story does not end here. Identification with the body results in identification with the mind along with its thoughts, emotions, ideas or opinions, which gathered around the idea of individuality. The fiction, called the individual mind, grows in stature as we began to identify with whatever came on the way. Just as iron-filings gather around a magnet and stick to it, thoughts, memories and notions gathered around the idea of the individual self. The game of false identification went on and on, as we continued to identify ourselves with external things like another person, a position, a social designation, a vocation and so on. Thus, the fictitious idea of individual self grew stronger and subsequently, the idea of a personality was born.

The individual self is an accumulation of ideas such as, 'I am this body, born in such and such family', 'my name is so and so,' 'I am educated, working as a teacher, doctor or engineer',' I am a socially respectable person', 'I am honest and responsible', and so on.

You took yourself to be a body born in a particular part of earth, in a certain family and engaged in a particular vocation; you took yourself to be a collection of certain ideas, opinions, likes and dislikes. Whenever any of these false identifications are threatened or challenged in any way, you feel that your own existence is threatened; you feel upset and your mind creates resistance to it in the form of negative emotions like anger, fear, hatred, resentment and the like.

This is the reason why people get upset, even angry, when faced with opinions contrary to their own. The mind immediately interprets it as a threat to its existence when somebody criticises or challenges its cherished thoughts, opinions or ideologies. The false and limited beliefs about us have given rise to the fiction of a small, transient, individual self, which begets suffering. The fiction has become so complete and 'real' that we completely identify with the fictitious role, which these beliefs have spun around us. We started looking at ourselves with the eyes of others and eventually believed us to be what others think of us. We absolutely forgot our inner being, as we tend to identify with the role that we are playing in this drama of life.

You can see it for yourself. Take a moment to close your eyes; sit up straight and just relax. Now ask yourself, who you really are. You might probably find yourself having answers as follows; like, you are a teacher, a student, a priest, a devotee, a doctor, an engineer, a manager, or, a father, a mother and so on.

These are but the roles assigned by life to your body-mind construct. It is perfectly okay to use them for the purpose of convenience in your daily life, but most often, we identify with the role so completely that we take it to be an identity of us. We forget that by thinking so about ourselves we are in reality identifying with a social mask and a transient station of life that can go away any moment. If all these roles, situations and positions are taken away from us, we continue to be who we are in our very essence. All these are situations and roles have hardly anything to do with what we really are at the core of our being. Ignorance of our true nature is the reason behind the false identifications.

As we evolve in our consciousness, slowly we begin to realize that this 'I' of ours is, in reality, pure consciousness. It is a knowing and being principle that knows the images floating on it; all the identifications with the images are just ideas, which have no reality behind them. It is only then, that we can abide in our unborn, intelligent nature; we abide in the inner sheath of 'I Am' and then, our self seems to be existing as this "I' consciousness. It is the original "I' consciousness which has been within us ever since we came into this world, and even before that. It is the witnessing presence. It is the principle of pure knowing and being that holds upon it the whole gamut of our experiences.

Again, at a certain stage of evolution, even this idea of 'I' disappears, as the 'I' consciousness dissolves in to self-aware silence of pure being. Our real Self has this non-self nature. It is the level existing beyond the thoughts. You can feel it as a sky-like emptiness that encompasses everything. This pure silence, as pure awareness of being, existing at the core of our existence, is our real essence.

When extroverted, this self-aware silence manifests as the cosmic 'I am' that exists in all beings as their 'I'. Even though it exists in the woman, it is not a woman. Even though it exists in a man, it is not a man. It is without form, color or any other attributes. We have superimposed different notions onto it. On this sense of pure being, we superimpose notions like "I am a man, a woman, an American, or an Indian", identifying with a body and a society where this body was born. Thus, a false self was born as a cluster of notions around the idea of an individual self.

Reality Beyond the Senses

Our sense organs help to maintain the show by generating false perceptions of the reality, which is one of the major causes of false identification with the body. The senses are called the deputy of the mind. They gather information from the surroundings with their limited capacity and generate false perceptions about the reality around us.

When we as pure consciousness ride the body at birth, we believe our senses as ourselves. As a result, we believe whatever information they supply to us, when what they actually do is distort the reality to paint a false picture for us due to their limited capacity. Our ears can hear only sounds that fall within the range of a certain frequency. Our eyes are only able to catch lights falling within a certain wavelength. All our audio-visual and sensory perceptions provide us with a very much inadequate, incomplete and inaccurate view of the universe. We humans have completely turned our backs to our real nature of inner light to live as the fiction generated by our senses and the mind.

Thanks to our faith on the information provided by the senses and the mind, we believe the perception generated by them as the 'reality'. However, the 'reality' experienced by the senses is not ultimately true. The reality that we experience in our daily life is, at best, a relative truth that holds good only for our daily behavioural purposes. A little knowledge of the modern science at the high-school level will convince you about the falsity of the information supplied by your senses.

Science tells us that, matter is condensed energy, and all matters in the physical universe operate on the various wavelengths of energy. It is important to understand that all that exists, whether seen or unseen, broken down into its simplest and most basic form consists of energy. Our sense organs do not allow us to perceive this universe as an energy-phenomenon.

Modern quantum physics has discovered that everything that exists really exists as waves of energy appearing and disappearing, coming in to and going out of existence. Everything means everything. Beginning from your body, your pet, your book, the stones, mountains, the Sun, the moon or the stars in the distant galaxy, all are made of energy in its purest form; energy appearing from and disappearing in to emptiness. The whole of the cosmos resembles a vast ocean of energy where numerous forms of waves are born and dying every moment. All the forms and phenomena of this creation are like waves, coming in to existence this moment and going out of existence a moment later, to be one with the ocean. We are no exception.

This cosmic energy ocean is the truth of this existence, where no division or demarcation exists. If our eyes would have the capacity to see a glimpse of this, the notion of individual self could hardly exist. In Quantum physics, consciousness is believed to exist as a unified field where everything is everything else. No boundaries exist. No 'this' or 'that', 'you' or 'me' exists except a pure field of consciousness, which exists as the essence of everything. All our bodies are inseparable parts of this energy-ocean.

. This quantum ocean of energy reminds us of the 'ocean of existence' described in the Hindu mythology. Also in the Buddhist scriptures, we find a mention to an 'ocean of becoming'.

Cosmic Dance of Energy

The body is a wave in the cosmic energy ocean of oneness. It is part of a unified field of energy. As we examine our body deeply, we find it to be a field of vibrant sensations. It is, as if, a miniature stage of the cosmic dance of the energy. Prana, the life force, is dancing on the background of pure consciousness, giving rise to thoughts on the background of silence. This energy dance is nicely described in the Hindu mythology as the dance of Shakti, the divine mother, on Shiva, who remains silent and still, lying down as a corpse, immersed in Samadhi. Shiva is the essence of pure consciousness, embodied. The divine mother as the cosmic 'I am' signifies the womb of creation. She is symbolic of the primal creative energy as the primordial thought of pure being and knowing, which manifests itself as every cell of the body.

Our physical and mental being, as we experience ourselves, is made of the thought energy. This primordial thought energy is dancing everywhere, manifesting itself in all other thoughts, experienced as the multifarious names and forms of this existence. This energy is operating in the creation, sustention and dissolution of all the sentient and insentient beings of this universe.

The Observer

Who is the spectator of this dance? Pure consciousness, as the witness, is experiencing this energy dance as the multifarious names and forms within it, through the sheath of 'I am'. Pure consciousness manifested as the cosmic ocean of pure 'I', is the observer. This is a fascinating reality. Consciousness, in one aspect is taking the form of flow energy to manifest the dance; in another aspect, consciousness as the witnessing energy witnesses the dance in silence.

There are infinite possibilities regarding where and how a particular wave might appear in an ocean. Just so, out of infinite possibilities in this cosmic ocean of energy, a specific manifestation in form takes place at a specific point of space and time, in the presence of consciousness as the observer.

Quantum physics have made a startling discovery. Scientists have found that an observed phenomenon is dependent on the person who observes it. It is you and I as the observer that determines the outcome of material manifestations in forms. In the everyday reality, the individual observer, as a tiny part of the Whole is observing another tiny part to which it is indivisibly connected through the Whole. The observer and the object of observation are part of one indivisible consciousness. Thus, the reality, seen from the individual perspective, is evidently relative, where observer is the part of the observed phenomena. Therefore, no observed phenomenon is an unalterable and concrete reality, as we normally believe. It is subject to change as the state of our consciousness changes.

The ultimate reality is more fascinating and mysterious where, the consciousness as an indivisible Whole is observing the parts contained within it. Here too, the observer is indivisibly connected to what it observes. Thus, the distinction between the seer, seen and seeing blurs out and ultimately vanishes in to the one indivisible unity of being. Modern science has come very close to what was revealed as the subjective experience of our ancient sages.

The Basis of Our Existence

Consciousness is the source of everything that is, was or will be. The whole universe is the play of pure consciousness. This is the supreme consciousness of God. This pure consciousness becomes coloured, as it is tinged with thoughts and imaginations, notions and beliefs. Consciousness is the essence that pervades, permeates and creates the body. It sustains nurtures and nourishes the body. It is this essential substance, which makes the body alive and operational on this earthly plane of existence.

Everything we experience, everything we feel and everything we do is an expression of our consciousness. Consciousness is the very basis of our existence. Consciousness of this body is felt as this body; consciousness of a pain is a pain, consciousness of joy is joy, consciousness of a taste is experienced as a taste and so on. Nothing can exist for us if we do not experience it within our consciousness. You might have finished a tasty meal without ever experiencing the taste, when you are preoccupied with a worry about some office job. The taste of the meal, the efficiency of your taste buds did not serve anything to make you experience the taste of the food since your consciousness was busy with another thing. Therefore, you see that the taste of the food is not an objective phenomenon existing independent of your consciousness.

Similarly, no experience in life exists outside of your consciousness. Consciousness is the one that experiences everything, and the mind is the one that interprets the experiences. We are consciousness, pure knowing and being principle, playing through the window of the matter vehicle, known as the body.

The Inner Guru

Our body, mind, thoughts, emotions and actions are happening on the level of the cosmic unconscious nature. Behind this unconscious and inert nature, there is one indivisible cosmic Self; our individual 'I Am' is a part of it. It is our intelligent and unborn nature. It holds the inner Guru in its bosom as the witnessing silence, just as the golden orb of the Sun holds the Sun within.

Infinite and unlimited consciousness is our real nature. It is the inner Sun, the inner Guru, which dispels the darkness of ignorance. This is the inner space within us where all the dualities, and consequently, all the conflicts vanish. It is a place of utter peacefulness. It is the domain of timelessness. It exists beyond the mind.

Though in the beginning, it seems to exist within the body, as you progress on the path, you will find that, in fact, all experiences of time and space are happening within it, in its presence. This witnessing consciousness is within and without of our body. It is one and indivisible, and is beyond cause and effect.

It is the cosmic essence of the primordial thought, 'I Am'. It underlies the whole creation. Yet, it is beyond the veil of 'I Am', beyond the thought of pure knowing and being. It is bliss absolute, eternal and non-decaying; it is the cosmic bliss, which sustains and nourishes the creation.

We are made of this God-essence, bliss essence, even when we are playing as veiled by the cocoon of individuality imposed by our body and mind. This God-essence within us acts as the inner Guru to banish the ignorance within us when we are awakened to it, when we are aware of it. This light of consciousness pervades our being. As we start to become conscious of this light, it becomes brighter and brighter ultimately to dispel all the false shadows and darkness. It is within each one of us. We are born with this treasure.

In Service of Inner Guru

Our born nature, the inert nature should be guided and ruled by our intelligent, unborn nature. If the inert nature is not under continuous supervision of our unborn nature, it may create havoc. Here comes the need for continuous awareness of our speech, actions and thoughts. This is another name of surrender; it is continuous surrender of our born nature to our unborn nature, which is of the nature of awareness.

Be compassionate with your body and mind, direct them with right understanding and be aware of their subtle workings. Then, these instruments will serve the inner light as the most obedient servants. Though the body and mind are not your real self, we can get nowhere by torturing our body and fighting with our mind. Many try to do so in an effort to establish mastery over them. It simply does not work that way. You have to befriend your body and mind and use them wisely. The Inner Guru is the friend of all beings. When you befriend your body and mind you align with the inner Guru.

If you are riding a car and happen to suffer by identifying with the car and its wheels, destroying the car is not the solution. Breaking away of the identification is the solution. That is possible by putting your attention not outside of the car, not on the car, but on yourself. You break away of the identification by looking at yourself, at your own being as you are. That is exactly what is to be done if you are to break away of the identification with the body. When you do that, by looking deeply in to mystery of your body and mind, you will know their subtle functioning. Then, they will become quiet and still, eager to serve the inner Guru.

Life Worshipping the Inner Guru

Life in all its manifestations is worshipping the inner Guru, through the gaps or silence existing between all thoughts, words, actions and events. In the very body of yours, life is worshipping the inner Guru. Many mysteries of the existence are hidden within this body. Though Inner Guru is present everywhere in this existence, we can access this light of pure being only within this body. Within the temple of the body is the hidden shrine of our consciousness. Once you study it deeply, understand it deeply, you will learn the art of opening its mysteries.

Our whole body, all the limbs, all the cells, the DNA and all the atoms are the access points of our Inner Guru as the inner light of bliss. This light of ever-present bliss permeates every atom of our body. From the tip of our toe to the top of our head, every cell is throbbing with the music of the energy of the consciousness. If we concentrate on any point, any cell, any atom of our body, we shall eventually be attuned with the consciousness that we are made of.

We can find the key to the infinite within the very body of ours. All we need is a shift of the attitude, a breaking away of the identification by persistent, thorough observation. In every cell of our body, the divine energy is silently worshipping the inner Guru in its inimitable way, the way of flow. When you attune yourself with this flow, a miracle will happen. Suddenly the flow will vanish, and your being will be dissolved in to the pure sky of non-decaying inner bliss. Suddenly all distinctions vanish and you melt away to be one with your inner Guru, the ever-present bliss as the essence of your being.

It happens in a rare moment when your body is relaxed, and the mind is peaceful and pure, uncontaminated and free from afflictions. Then, you will find that it is not the body, which contains the Inner Guru. It is really the other way round. Your body and all the others are contained within it. Inner Guru is the very container and content of this body. Then this very body becomes the gateway to Nirvana. Then, you will find that body and other objects that are floating in this light are not as real as the light is. All the earthly solidities are no more real than a thought or a dream existing in our consciousness. They have no reality apart from our consciousness.

Then and only then you will truly appreciate the body as a gift from the divine. In fact, there is nothing wrong with the body. All that was wrong was born through our identification with it. Identification with the body landed us in to the misery of Samsara. As we break away of the identification, the false concept of who we are melts away in to the serene and pure bliss of being. It is then when we understand that Samsara and Nirvana are two different facets of the same ever-present reality that alone exists.

Chapter Four

THE MIND OF GOD

"Nada is found within. It is a music without strings, which plays in the body. It penetrates the inner and the outer and leads you away from illusion." --*Kabir*

Understanding the mystery of sound and soundlessness is necessary to know the mind of God or the God consciousness existing within you. A backdrop of soundlessness exists behind all the names, forms and sounds of this creation. This background of soundlessness is not absolute absence of sound. It is silence throbbed with the cosmic melody of being, unheard by ordinary human ears. This soundless sound is our inner Guru. This substratum of the soundless sound holds all the sounds of this universe. This universe is woven by the threads of sounds on the background of soundless sound of existence. We need to study, contemplate and realize these twin aspects of sound and soundlessness, if we want to realize God within.

Sounds: The Creative Energy of God

Our ancients believed that sound is the basic ingredient of this creation. In ancient India, great sages metaphorically described this creative sound-principle as a feminine aspect of the divine. They named this great goddess of creation as *Vak Devi*. We have an entire Upanishad dedicated to her. *Vak*, in Sanskrit, is ordinarily translated as the sound that carries a meaning within it. However, it has a wider connotation. The word *Vak* refers to the whole range of vibrations including all audible and inaudible sounds. It also refers to the subtlest vibration in the mind manifested as the thoughts. *Devi* comes from the root word 'Div' that, in Sanskrit, means the illumining principle.

Vak Devi is described as the Goddess of sound; it is the divine principle that illumines all the sounds to make them manifest. It is the divine principle that creates and illumines all the energy vibrations of this existence to make them manifest as various names and forms. The sages believed that it is *Vak*, the sound vibrations at the subtlest level, which manifested itself as the names and forms of this creation. Hence, sounds are sacred. No wonder, that, the ancients believed in the power of the mantras, the sound vibrations capable of manifesting things or situations on the physical plane of existence.

Vak Devi, in her another name, is Saraswati, which means the flowing essence; symbolically she is also portrayed as a river. It is said that she flowed as the primordial divine sound and manifested herself as this universe. She is the river of consciousness. She flows and manifests herself as different forms, and holds them all within. Hence, *Vak Devi* is also hailed as the 'Jagad-dhatri', which, in Sanskrit, means the aspect of the God that holds, nurses, nourishes and sustains the universe.

The sages hailed her as the one who creates and protects every being. She is painted as a great musician holding the harp, a stringed musical instrument in her hands. In another hand, she holds the book of wisdom. She is the eternal Guru. She is the very substratum of our being. She is the soundless sound of existence that permeates and sustains the Universe. All the sounds, and consequently, everything that exists, emanates from, exists upon and dissolves back in to this soundless sound of existence. She can lead a devoted seeker from the noise of this material plane to the transcendental silence of pure being.

In our body, sounds are produced as speech through the throat and tongue. Our ancients believed that mastery over the tongue could bring them mastery over the universe. They considered the tongue to be the seat of *Vak-Devi*, the great goddess of consciousness. Keeping the tongue under vigilance was important to make the seat of the great goddess pure. So, as an integral part of their spiritual practices, the ancient yogis incorporated practices such as observation of silence, being mindful and reticent in speech, and practices such as taking the right food or fasting.

Universe: The Tapestry of Sound

Everything in this universe is made of sound on the background of silence, just as words are written on a white paper. As the physicists would tell us, anything and everything in this universe is made of the vibration or movement of subatomic particles, which also are capable of manifesting of wave. At a subtler level, everything in this universe exists in the form of vibration or waves. Some of these vibrations manifest as sounds, some as forms, colours or even thoughts. The ancient seers believed that every vibration produces a subtle sound.

Given the limited nature of receptivity of our ears, we can not hear all the sound vibrations that exist in our universe just as we are incapable of seeing the full spectrum of electromagnetic waves. The ranges of ordinary audible sounds that exist in our surroundings are coarsest manifestation of sound. Human hearing lies in the range of frequency between sixteen to twenty thousand hertz, approximately. Consequently, we can perceive very little of the music going on in and around us. Throughout the outer space, there are many sounds such as the hums emitted by the movement of the planets, the gaseous interactions taking place within the Sun and the pulsating rhythms of the stars. These sounds resemble our earthly music. Though we can not hear these sounds, thanks to the blanket of the air in the atmosphere, we are affected, nevertheless, by this cosmic music of the spheres.

We too are musical beings. Music is continuously going on within our own brain, within our body. Electroencephalograph (EEG), the instrument used to measure the bioelectric impulses produced by the brain, registers low frequency sine waves. Modern scientists have discovered that these waves produced by our brain actually belong to the notes of the musical scale. Since the human ear is unable to register sounds below the frequency of sixteen hertz, we can not perceive this music going on within our own body.

Music is a rhythmic vibration of sound. There is a rhythm in the functioning of every organ of the body. The heart beating, the blood coursing through the veins, the lungs expanding and contracting, all these functions are evidently vibratory in nature, happening in a certain rhythm in an on-off sequence. We are musical beings, with our body itself behaving as a musical instrument. It is precisely the reason why music has so profound an effect on our body and mind, no matter, which country or culture we belong. Music can uplift our mood, stimulate or inspire us to work, or can lull us in to sleep. Sound can also create disharmony or irritation if its vibration does not match our own. As we all know, certain music can make us sad, depressed or irritated. Sound of a waterfall or a mountain stream can soothe the tired body and mind, while the sound of a generator can make us tired.

Ancient civilizations and religions were familiar with the use of sound to balance and maintain health from within as well as to create harmony in the environment. Mantras are subtle music. For thousands of years bells and chanting have been used in the Tibetan monasteries, Buddhist and Hindu temples. It was one of the most powerful tools for healing the human body and spirit. This whole universe is a wonderful tapestry of sound embroidered on the background of soundlessness.

Journey from Sound to Soundlessness

Our ancient sages had known the full spectrum of the sound vibrations that might be perceptible to a human being. They classified those sounds in to four categories:

Para was the name of the transcendental sound; it is the soundless sound, which is beyond ordinary perception. *Pashyanti* was the name of the visible sound, which we ordinarily experience as a feeling or a mental picture. *Madhyama* was the name of the sound in between, which we experience as thoughts and words; and *Vaikhari* was the name of the audible sound, which is expressed as speech. Each level of sound corresponds to a certain plane of existence, a certain state of consciousness. Our ability to experience the different levels of sound depends upon the refinement of our consciousness.

From the point of ordinary perception, the first level of sound is that which falls within the audible range. It is called the *Vaikhari-Vak*. It is the grossest level of speech, heard through the ears. When sound comes out through the mouth as spoken syllables it is named as *Vaikhari*. The word 'V*aikhari'* literally means the flowering. When the subtle seeds of thoughts flowers as the speech, action, name and form in the material plane of existence the vibration at this level is known as the *Vaikhari*. Therefore, '*Vaikhari*' is the sound that has manifested itself on the material plane.

Then, we have the inaudible sounds. There are also the finer sounds that exist as a thought prior to expression. These types of sounds are called the *Madhyama-Vak*.

Madhyama is the intermediate and unexpressed state of sound, whose seat is in the heart. The word *Madhyama* means "in between" or "the middle". It exists in between the formation of a thought as an idea, feelings or image and its expression on the material level as speech or action. It is on this level that we notice our thoughts. Therefore, '*Madhyama*' is the sound that manifested itself on the mental plane of consciousness.

On the third level, sound leaves its audible nature and manifests as a feeling, a wordless idea or some visual imagery. It is very subtle vibration or sound. It is called *Pashyanti-Vak. Pashyanti* in Sanskrit means, "That which can be seen or visualized". At this level, sound possesses qualities, such as color and form. Yogis who have inner vision can intuitively perceive these qualities in sound. At the level of *Pashyanti-Vak*, the differences between languages do not exist because *Pashyanti-Vak* is intuitive in nature and it is constructed beyond the rigidly defined linguistic form or framework. Therefore, *Pashyanti* is the sound that manifest at a deeper and subtler mental plane of consciousness.

On the level four, sound leaves even its visual nature to remain only as a potential. It is the potential ground of all possible sounds. It is unmanifest, *Abyakta*, in Sanskrit. It is called the *Para-Vak. Para-Vak* is the transcendental sound.

It is this that they called the soundless sound. It is beyond the reach of mind and intelligence. It can not be defined by words. You may have an idea about it by listening to the silence that follows as a kinesthetic experience at the end of chanting "Om". At the level of individual, *Para-Vak* is the sound of your soul. At the level of the cosmic Whole, this is the soundless sound of Existence, which is our inner Guru.

Soundless sound of existence has given birth to all the sounds. Consider a seed, a sprout, and a tree. They can beautifully portray the array of sounds in the existence: the tree as the first kind of manifested sound, the sprout as the second kind and the seed as the third kind of visible sound. Beyond this range of manifested sounds, lies the unmanifest essence of the seed that portrays the fourth level, the soundless sound.

The whole macrocosmic universe of our thoughts and experiences are a projection of sound vibrations of different frequencies. All levels of our existence are constituted of these four kinds of sound vibrations. Our actions and speech belong to the first level of sound, the sounds that manifest on the grossest level. Our thoughts belong to the second level of knowable sound. Our feeling belong to the third; and beyond the level of action, speech, thoughts and feelings, rests the unmanifest essence of our being, our soul, which is the transcendental. Moving from the sounds, our grosser being, to the subtlest inner presence of soundlessness could be a great experience, a journey worth taking.

The Bridge between Individual and God

The soundless sound is the very substratum of Existence. It exists as a background of creation. Though we call it the soundless sound, it is never really a sound audible to human ears; nor is it an inert silence. It throbs with the melody of a silent cosmic presence, a witnessing presence, which our inner Guru is.

The whole universe emerges from it, exists on it and ultimately dissolves back in to it. All the creatures on earth, the book you are holding on, the stone and trees in the garden, the stars in the sky or a supernova, everything exists on this background of soundlessness. This background is very important basis for any particular vibration of sound to exist.

For the letters to exist, the background of paper is as important as the ink with which you write. Just so, it is as important to understand this soundless, silent background of our being, as it is, to understand the sounds. For a harmonious and holistic living, we can not neglect either of them. On this background of the soundless sound of existence, this universe exists as a sound-phenomenon. If all the forms of this universe were letters, the background where they are written, is this vast space of silence.

This mysterious silence on the background of sounds, the great void on the background of forms, also represents something hidden deep within us. Be it a bird, an animal, a tree, or a river, a lake or a mountain, the soundless sound of existence reverberates within it. It exists within all sentient and non-sentient beings, creating them with its mysterious power of creation, sustaining them with its power of nourishment until the time comes when the body goes to dissolution, embracing the natural law of existence.

This soundless sound is also called the *Unstruck* sound of existence, which can not be perceived by the ears of flesh. It could be perceived through inner ears, depending on the degree of one's capability to attune to the inner world. As you progress on the path, initially, it might be heard as a buzzing, a ringing of the bell, as the sound of the thunder, or the sound of waves at the shore of an ocean. It is sometimes heard as the distant sound of a flute, sometimes as the melodious sound of the *Sehnai*, an Indian musical instrument that produces music of celebration.

This soundless sound is the silent music of celebration, ceaselessly going on in this existence. It is the unfolding of grace in your being when you stop for a moment to be silent and attune your being with it. Some calls this sound the Nada Brahman, the soundless sound of the Infinite. People in various religious traditions have called it by names such as Om, or Aum, or the Omkar, or Amen.

Nevertheless, no human utterance can exactly simulate this soundless sound of existence because it is the un-struck sound. It is produced without one object striking another. All sounds in existence are produced through the striking of one object with another, or by friction of two objects. For example, the sounds produced by your vocal cords are created by friction of air with the vocal cord, as you breathe out and the air goes out. Only this soundless sound is produced by itself. Hence, it is called *Anahata*, the unstruck.

By attuning to this soundless sound your body becomes peaceful, the mind tranquil, intellect melted in the light of the inner Guru, and ultimately, the sense of individuality merges in to the eternal silence of pure being. This is a state of grace impossible to describe in words.

Make yourself available to the river of grace that is already flowing within your being. Almost all the ancient scriptures sing the glory of this soundless sound of existence. In the Bible, they say, "In the beginning was the Word. And the Word was with God, and the Word was God." What is this Word? It is this soundless sound. It is the inner Guru. Witnessing silence is its nature. It is that which created this creation from its own essence.

Hatha Yoga Pradipika, an ancient treatise to Yoga sings the glory of this soundless sound in the following way; "Salutation to the soundless sound of existence, which is the inner guide and the inner life, the dispenser of happiness to all. It is the inner Guru. One who is devoted to the inner Guru, the soundless sound, the inner music, obtains the highest bliss."

Everything in Nature is this song of silence celebrating itself. The passing breeze, the gushing river, the starry night, the floating white clouds, the Sun, the moon all are a symphony of silence, made of this soundless sound, the primordial vibration of Existence. Anything that exists makes this humming sound in the backdrop of pure silence. That is why being close to Nature is so refreshing for the tired body and exhausted mind. That is why the energy of silence is so life giving. When you are attuned with the silence of Nature, you automatically make yourself open to this soundless sound of existence.

The Golden Light of Being

This soundless sound of existence is the song of silence. It is the soundless music, the fragrance of godliness within. It resonates within your very being as your Inner Guru. It is the sound of eternity. It is the light of witnessing. It is the golden light of being. Behind the incessant noise of the body and the ceaseless chatter of the mind, is hidden this luminous presence of the golden silence as the witnessing presence within us. This luminous Sun is carrying transcendental silence in its bosom. Within the sheath of the one and indivisible cosmic Self, it holds this core of silence as pure being. This silence allows the entire universe to be. Learning to attune to this silence is the essence of all spiritual practices.

Knowing the Intimate Nature of Silence

The word 'silence' usually carry very negative or pessimistic connotation for some people. People usually understand it as indicating some emptiness, a sad or hollow state of affair. This wrong understanding is prevalent because there are very few people who really have experienced the blissful silence of their inner being. At the most superficial level, we know silence as the absence of noise. Though that may be the case in the beginning, as you learn to attune with silence, slowly, you move from the silence of environment to the silence of your body; from silence of your body to the silence of your mind; from silence of your mind to the silence of your soul. It is at this level that you touch the most blissful essence of your being and your silence is overflowed with joy, love and peace. It is the Life itself, the unborn and never dying essence of your soul. Though it exists within every plant, animal and insentient things in the Nature, surrounding them with its refreshing and rejuvenating freshness, only human beings are privileged to enjoy the mystery of it.

Silence Beyond Witnessing: The Mind of God

When the incessant chattering noise of the mind stops, the soundless sound is uncovered within your being. Beyond the soundless sound of existence, beyond the level of individual witnessing, there exists the pure silence, the mind of God. When your mind is absolutely at rest, when your awareness is withdrawn to your inner being, a rare moment comes. At that most precious moment, the pure silence of your being reveals itself. This pure silence is even beyond witnessing. It is the infinite mind, the mind of God. Our inner journey from sound to soundlessness will not be complete until we realize this pure silence within our being, as our being.

When you experience God as the essence of your inner being, you come to the summit of your journey. You become peaceful, happy and utterly content within. This gentle, loving, inner peace and silence already exists within you. It stays calm, peaceful and silent in midst of all the turmoil of life. When your mind becomes subtle and pure you can spontaneously be aware of this sacred silence within you. We all carry this silent sanctuary of the heart, sometimes buried under oblivion in the chaotic space of daily living. This place exists much beyond the chatter of the mind, much beyond the feelings and emotions. Nothing from outside can touch it and this place is never lost, however remote your mind might have taken yourself from it. It is a realization of pure being. It is the essence of Godliness within us. In essence, the awareness of our being is the silence itself. This silence permeates everything. This silence allows us to be free. This is the very centre of our being. It is the beauty that never fades.

This mysterious and eternal reality is waiting to reveal itself within you. This is something that, no matter what has occurred in your life, has never changed. Days come and go, years come and go, lives come and go, but the eternal silence of your being remains the same. It is not your silence. You are it. This silence is your very being.

When this silence is outgoing, it flows out and exists as the witness to the world of name and form; it becomes the golden Sun, the soundless sound of existence. When this silence is drawn inwards, witnessing too is gone; then this luminous sun, the soundless sound melts away to nothingness revealing the sky of your being in its core as pure silence. This silence beyond witnessing exists as supreme emptiness, which is the womb of creation, the ground of all possibilities. It is the very essence of your being.

You may get the feel of it this very moment, if you are ready. Stop reading for a moment and close your eyes. Let go of the thoughts, the imagination, the emotions; let go of everything, and see what is left. Try to feel that inner core of your being, the inner silence that is always within you, below the level of your moods, your emotions and your thoughts. There is nothing to find out, nothing to imagine, and nothing to anticipate. Just listen with your whole being to what is here, now.

Could you feel, even for a split moment, the pure silence of your inner being? Could you feel the space where no thought, no emotion, no feeling, except for a deep feeling of pure beingness was present? Then you have tasted it. Pure Silence resides within you. It is not just the absence of sound, or lack of noise. It is the ground, the basis of your very being. It is awareness of being in its purest form.

People use to spend their entire life running away from this silence, fearing this silence, covering this silence with this and that, keeping them preoccupied with thousands of means and media. People spend their entire life denying what is more intimate to them than their very breath, their very heartbeat. Yet, this is the place of our true rest. This is the place synonymous with inner peace. This place nurtures our body, mind and soul. This is the space where you are inseparably one with the mind of God. All the existence, everything that is, all the matter and energy and all the thoughts are contained in this pure silence. Very few are aware of this silent core within them. It heals the body, rejuvenates the mind.

Your body and mind are automatically ushered in to the core of inner silence everyday, though unconsciously, when you are lulled to sleep. Nature has automatically designed the rejuvenating silence of sleep everyday for your weary body and tired mind. Sleep is Mother Nature's automatic protective mechanism for the maintenance of your body and mind, when you get respite from the activities of the body and compulsive chatter of the mind.

It has been proven through modern research that, if a person is deprived from sleep, first she will feel weak, indicating the loss of physical strength; then, she will be easily irritable, gradually loosing her patience, clarity, balance and mental poise. Ultimately, madness and even death might occur if she persists with the experiment. During the entire period of sleep, the silent phase of dreamless sleep is most important. At this phase of sleep, the natural healing takes place.

However, sleep is just an unconscious defence mechanism to ensure the correct functioning of the body and mind. For awakening your inner Guru, you have to learn to enter the silence of your inner being, consciously. The power of silence is invincible. Silence is the food for our soul. By learning to attune to your inner silence, you automatically attune with your inner Guru. Learning to attune to this silence will bring peace, truth, love and a thousand blessings to you. When you are able to attune to this inner silence, you may experience a mysterious phenomenon; you will find this silence to emerge out of your being like a clear stream of water to lull your objective mind, and ultimately this river of silence will surround, pervade and permeate your entire being, taking it in its loving embrace. It is an ultimate experience of blessedness.

Chapter Five

PREPARATION FOR AWAKENING

"Our life is shaped by our mind; we become what we think. Joy follows a pure mind like a shadow that never leaves." – *Dhammapada*

Did you ever observe a gardener working in his garden? A wise gardener knows the importance of preparing the soil for the growth of the plant and blossoming of the flowers. He knows how to bring forth flowers of immaculate beauty from the dirty soil. If you neglect the soil, plants will not get sufficient nutrition and flowers will not blossom. Our body and mind are the soil, which, if properly prepared, will bring forth wonderful inner lotuses when the inner Sun rises, dispelling eons of ignorance.

To prepare the soil for awakening, we need to train the body and the mind. We need to develop some inner faculties. Firstly, we must take care of the body, nourish it and keep it active. Through wholesome and nutritious diets, and practices of yoga and awareness, we make the body fit for integration with the whole. We should not neglect the body, nor should we pamper it. There must be a healthy balance in everything we do. So long as the body is not in perfect health, you will be caught in the body-consciousness alone; then it will be very difficult to transcend the body and move to deeper levels of the consciousness.

Next, we need to take care of our mind. The mind is continuously busy in running shows, one after another, by producing a ceaseless stream of thoughts, images and emotions. We need practices to have a calm, stable and serene mind. Only a mind that can remain in deep rest can help to reveal the divinity within.

If you want to connect with your Inner Guru, you need to attune to that state. As we know, it is a state of infinite peace, harmony, joy, gratitude and fulfilment. It is a realm of infinite abundance and perfection. Moreover, it is the eternal present, a realm of here and now. If you want to make yourself attuned to this state, the mind needs to be quiet, peaceful and in a state of harmony with all that exists. If our mind is clouded and restless, we will fail to find the inner light even when the light always exists within.

Most of the masterpieces of arts and music flow from a place unknown to mind. The poets, artists and musicians have acknowledged this fact throughout the ages. It is a place called no-mind, which is a state of spontaneous meditation. It happens when the thinking capacity is completely at rest. It is a moment of absolute inner clarity, when wisdom, insights and creativity from the beyond peeps in and flows through the channel of the mind. This realm of no-mind is the realm of the inner Guru.

Understanding the Mind

The first lesson in preparing for the awakening is to understand your mind so thoroughly that you know all its hidden motives. We should know the subtle ways of operation of the mind. We need to know the reasons why it behaves in a particular fashion in certain situations. Understanding gives us power. A thorough understanding of the mind is necessary to befriend it and eventually to master and train it to be at the service of the inner Guru.

Nevertheless, our knowledge must be rooted in our inner experience. Theoretical knowledge will not do. Knowledge, only when received at the level of experience, becomes the power. Knowledge, if not grounded in the inner silence of being, only serves to increase useless chatter in the mind, obscuring the light. We need to learn to observe our mental realm to understand it.

Mind is in Search for Bliss

Our sense organs are the deputies of the mind. They are moving in a thousand and one directions in the outside world. The mind itself is running in every direction creating thousands of thoughts and emotions. If you observe, you will see that your mind always moves in a polarity. It moves between joy and sorrow, between hopes and despair, between exhilaration and depression, between the past and the future. It is always on the move. The mind moves in the search of joy.

The mind lives in a sense of perpetual lack or insufficiency. Limitless bliss is our real nature and mind is always in search of that bliss in limited things because the very nature of mind is limitedness. Objects of the world, limited as they are by nature, can never provide us total fulfilment. Limited things can never lead us to unlimited and permanent satisfaction. Therefore, the mind is never satisfied with what it gets. As soon as one desire is satisfied, it gets up to run after another desire. Everywhere in life, in every field, social, cultural, religious or professional, you will notice this sense of lack or insufficiency in people, if you have eyes to see. Somewhere it is pronounced and somewhere it runs very subtly behind the daily chores as a sense of boredom.

People seem to fill this sense of lack by various means, such as buying a new gadget, planning to travel to a place of interest, going to see a movie, participating in a sensational event or sports, participating in some festivity, doing some work of charity or service, and so the list goes on. At a higher level of consciousness, this feeling of insufficiency manifests as a search to find the meaning of life. This urge may manifest as a constant drive to find a new spiritual technique, search for a new master or joining one after another retreat or workshop.

There is nothing wrong in doing so. In fact, any desire, material or spiritual, is, in essence, only a search for the limitless bliss of our being. Desires can be a powerful tool for evolution, only if you live your life in an alert and aware manner. Desire for bliss can lead you to higher and higher realms of your being provided you are aware enough to see through the veil of it. That, which binds, has the potential to make you free, if you are aware.

If you are aware of the play of your own mind, if you can observe it as you are observing somebody else, you will find yourself caught in a series of moments of fleeting joys, one after another. You will find yourself trying to get hold of a moment of joy only to lose it a moment later, as another desire pops up. You will see that huge gulfs of dissatisfaction and boredom exist between the brief moments of joy and celebration in life.

Bliss is Within You

When you get thorough understanding of the working of your own mind, you will find that, the temporary things of the world only tire you in the long run, never giving you a lasting satisfaction; and in the end, they always leave you where you were in the beginning. Ultimately, you realize that there is no bliss other than the original bliss of your being. If you can not withdraw your attention from the external objects, you can not move inward because they will go on pulling you from the outside.

The basic understanding lies in the fact that, a desired object never creates a joy that originally was not within you. What the desired objects, places or people really do is that, they make your mind's chatter stop for a very brief moment to reveal the inner Sun of bliss, which is your real nature, always existing in the core of your being behind the clouds of incessant thoughts and storms of emotions.

However, as we all know, the excitement and joy from the fulfilment of a desire does not last very long. As soon as the experience ends, or the objects become old, the joy of the excitement begins to fade away, and the same object becomes incapable of holding the mind to keep it quiet.

The temporary joy of fulfilment of a desire disappears, as the mind becomes restless again with the clouds of thoughts and desires running on your being. The mind runs after new excitements and life becomes boring once again, as it was before, until your mind finds a new something or someone to keep itself busy with, in expectation for bliss to happen again. Thus, the mind goes on and on, never resting for a moment, creating a veil of continuous inner chatter to cloud the light of bliss that is our original nature. We experience this inner shadow as boredom, lack, dissatisfaction and restlessness.

When you see this clearly, you have no option but to step out of this seemingly perpetual wheel of desiring, having the object of your desire, being dissatisfied or disillusioned with what you have, and again finding yourself desiring something else, to fill the feeling of lack. When you gain knowledge over your mind at the level of your own experience, it gives you tremendous authority over the instrument that the mind is. Only then can you make good use of this wonderful and powerful instrument for the benefit of yourself and others. Otherwise, this instrument takes over you, continuously producing shadows and darkness in your being to make your daily life boredom at the best, and misery at its worst.

Barrier to Experience Limitless Bliss

Paradoxically, mind itself creates the barrier to the unlimited bliss it wants to experience! The incessant chatter of the mind and its continuous movement to the past and future clouds the bliss of our being. We need to understand that the mind can never experience limitless bliss because it itself is limited by nature.

Moreover, the mind is a storehouse of memory, an accumulation of the past moments. Consequently, it does not like to live in the present. It is always busy with the past memories, pleasant as well as unpleasant ones. It knows nothing about what the future is going to be. It only projects the recycled memories in the future, in the form of false hopes, expectations, fear and anxiety.

It is precisely the reason why, living in your mind, living as your mind, can never bring you genuine bliss and fulfilment. When you are convinced of the fact that the mind as a thinking mechanism can not lead you to the perpetual bliss of your being, then you will make an effort to step out of the chatter of the mind. Though you can use your thinking capacity in a constructive way for the benefit of yourself and others, continuous and compulsive thinking drains out tremendous amount of energy, and fatigues you in the end. Almost every one of us has noticed how tiring it feels when an obstinate thought would not want to go in spite of your earnest effort to get rid of it. It comes back repeatedly to wreak havoc on you.

All our thoughts are either a memory of the past or an imagination about the future. In reality, past does not exist anymore. It has ended completely and the future does not exist at all; it simply has not happened yet. Both the past and the future are only a part of our thoughts and memories; they only exist in our mind and not in the reality. When we see this clearly, we try to shift our focus of attention on what is happening in the present moment.

Living our life with our awareness totally focussed on the present moment is a wonderful way to stop the thinking mind. This non-thinking mind is the doorway to reach the spontaneous, ever-present bliss of our being. Observation of the mind is necessary to come out of the stream of compulsive thoughts.

Observing the Mind

Ordinarily, you live at the periphery of your being and think yourself as your body and the mind, including all its thoughts and emotions. Countless thoughts of daily trivia, worries and anxieties, hopes and expectations, anticipation and frustration run in your being. They run continuously to ravage your being without your permission. You remain chained by your own thoughts and habits. Man lives his whole life as the prisoner of his own mind.

Most of us do not have the capacity to detach ourselves from our obstinate mental chatter, fixed ideas or intellectual standpoint. We deeply associate with our thoughts to the extent that we often completely identify our being with them. Thus, we are forced to act upon to serve the whims of our mind. This is clearly a state of bondage.

How do you break away from this bondage? How do you step out of the mind? There is a way. Witnessing is the way. Let us explain, how. First, let us know, how you identify with a thought. Suppose a thought of anger peeps in your mind. In the absence of witnessing, you identify with this thought in a split second with the help of further thoughts such as "This thought is mine", and then "This is me". The next thought that follows is "I am angry". Evidently, the subsequent thought would be regarding taking action on the object of anger, which will make you act upon the thought. Thus, identification with a thought can make you miserable.

To break out of this bondage, you bring witnessing in the scene. Witnessing gives you the power to witness a thought, as and when it arises. Witnessing gives you the power to know a thought just as a thought, without assigning a label of "me" or "mine" to it. Witnessing gives you the power to observe a thought objectively as a passing phenomenon in your being. The same "I" which use to identify with the thoughts as "me" or "mine", can stand apart and aloof from the thoughts, and remain a witness to it. When your "I" becomes a witness to the passing phenomena of body, mind, thoughts and emotions, it becomes aligned to the transcendental consciousness. Then it assumes the nature of the spirit and it is then called the 'soul'. You, as the soul, are ever aligned with your inner Guru, the infinite Self, and the infinite energy of pure consciousness.

When you observe your own mind as a witness, you will be astonished to find how we unconsciously choose our destiny, our sorrow and suffering and also our joy and good fortune, by our unconscious choice of thoughts. Observation of the mind will make you free from the slavery of mind. It will make you free from the compulsive chatter of the mind. It will put you on a throne above the mind.

You are not Your Thoughts

Thoughts are nothing but recycled ideas, notions and imaginations that come back repeatedly in different disguises in different situations. They appear on the sky of our consciousness as a stream of words and images replayed, or reproduced by our mind, which mostly gathers them from an external situation. The mind gathers these ideas or imaginations from our parents, cultures, educational backgrounds, media or the society; then it recycles them to fit them in our specific life situation.

Though thoughts seem to appear automatically on your consciousness making you a helpless spectator, you are not as helpless as it seems to be. You are free to choose your thoughts. Your helplessness started from identifying with something, which is not yourself. You think that you are one with these thoughts. Your identification with the thoughts begins with the false belief such as, "This thought is me or it is mine." This identification makes you miserable by making you experience the slavery of the thoughts and emotions. You forget that you have the choice, regarding which thought you want to welcome and which to reject.

As you learn to observe your mental realm, you find that, most of the time this stream of words and images goes on without a purpose; like shadows, they produce a veil clouding the inner sky. You find that thoughts come to us, stay for a while and go away. This is true even for the thoughts of most obstinate nature. You will notice that your mental movie changes continuously. Bubbles of thoughts and emotions are rising, floating for a while, and then, changing their forms. The most persistent thought of yesterday are gone today, leaving nothing but a memory; just so, the most persistent thought of today will become 'nothing' in the future.

You are the one that remains constant among this flux. You are the one that perceives these thoughts and emotions appearing and disappearing in the inner sky of your being. Gradually, you discover the truth that you are not your thoughts.

This insight becomes a valuable weapon in dealing with the unwanted thoughts and emotions. You realize that you have the freedom of not to act upon every thought that the mind displays on your being. As you learn to distance yourself from the mental movie of thoughts and emotions, you gain the power to ignore a thought. There might be instances when an angry thought floats up on the screen of mind, you watch it from a distance as an aloof onlooker, and subsequently choose to ignore it. It gives you tremendous freedom, freedom to rest and relax in the pristine purity and peace of the sky of your inner being. Gradually, you learn to abide in a space, which is much away from the outer periphery of mind where thoughts reign. It gives you freedom to remain undisturbed, whatever the situation may be on the outside.

Thoughts are Energy

Thoughts are tiny energy pockets in consciousness that wait to be manifested in reality as actions, things, people and situations. Physics has proved long before that energy can not be destroyed in this universe. They can be transformed at the best. There is no exception to this natural law also in the domain of our thought energy. Like any other form of energy in Nature, it can bring good or bad, wanted or unwanted outcomes within our body, mind and environment, depending on how wisely or unwisely we harness it.

A thought can be transformed, either to thoughts of another kind, or to a material reality. Einstein's famous equation $E=mc^2$, where E is used to denote the energy, m is used to denote the mass of the matter and c indicates the speed of light, suggests that matter and energy are mutually convertible. From this, we can easily infer that thought energy too could be transformed in to material reality.

We are born with a reservoir of energy within us that is million times more potent than the atomic energy. This is the energy of our consciousness. This energy is neutral in nature. Like any other form of energy in Nature, it can bring good or bad, wanted or unwanted outcomes within our body, mind and environment, depending on how wisely or unwisely we harness it.

Thoughts Make the Destiny

Thoughts are the blueprint of the movie of life. The energy of consciousness, when focussed on a thought, makes it a perception in reality. A thought cherished for a long time with enough intensity of focus manifests as the reality by the energy of consciousness. When a thought or idea recurs repeatedly, it forms a habitual pattern and this pattern is known as a conditioning. When we store these gathered ideas in our consciousness, our mind becomes conditioned to think, act or behave in a certain manner. When a habitual pattern of thought is established, we unconsciously believe it to be an unalterable, absolute truth. When you believe a thought to be a truth, you behave accordingly with strong emotions of like and dislike attached towards a particular thing, person or situation. Thoughts, thus, form a habit; habits form action, which manifests as a situation, or a series of situations. This ultimately comes to be believed as the destiny.

However, the chain starts by a tiny seed of thought in your mind, unconsciously chosen most of the time. Mind is mechanical in nature and it brings forth many unwanted thoughts that might be self-destructive in nature. The mind is also vulnerable to suggestions from the world outside. Suggestions come from the friends, relatives or the mass media. These suggestions, sometimes happens to be negative in nature. The mind readily accepts them in unawareness, embraces them as its own, and believes them to be true, to its own detriment.

The thoughts and feelings generated, attracted and cherished by our mind are like the seeds. These seed vibrations manifest as sprouts and plants on the next level of consciousness as speech, things, body, actions and the outer environment. Thoughts carrying the emotions of worries, fear, guilt, anxiety, jealousy and hatred are unwholesome in nature, that create the reality of fearful or stressful situations, sadness, estrangement and many diseases of the body.

Most of the time people are not even aware of creating an unwanted outcome or a situation by weaving an unwholesome thought in their mind. It is also worth knowing that in the realm of thoughts, like attracts like. A thought of worry, fear or lack will attract many such thoughts already floating in the cosmic mind released by others, strengthening your negative attitude, bringing the experience of misery.

Similarly, a thought of joy, love, purity or abundance will attract similar thoughts from the cosmic repository, strengthening your own thoughts of similar kind, to manifest as the good fortune. If the thoughts are of the pure and wholesome nature, sprouts and plants of pure and auspicious things will grow on the level of your body, mind and environment.

You are the Choice-Maker

You are the choice maker about whether you would like to entertain a certain thought, or not. Always remind yourself that you have the power to choose your thoughts, and through your thoughts, your life. Consciously choose joy and not sorrow; choose abundance, not lack; choose kindness, not cruelty; choose health and not disease; choose peace instead of war. Though this may sound obvious, if you are constantly mindful of your thoughts, you will be surprised to learn that your mind often goes the wrong way, by cultivating unconscious, destructive inner dialogue. Always choose good things for yourself and for others.

To be able to make choices regarding your thoughts, you will have to be able to see your thoughts as a witness, instead of identifying with them. The beginning of inner freedom is having an awareness of your thoughts. It is the ability to observe your thoughts objectively, without being involved in them. Ability of witnessing your thoughts has many benefits. It gives you freedom to choose or deny any thought created within your mind, or coming from some external sources. This ability to witness creates a centre within you where you can stand aloof, no matter what happens outside. It gives you the ability to stay connected with your inner Guru, who is the eternal witness. When you realize that you are free to choose your thoughts, you are in a position to claim your right back from the mind. This is the beginning of mental mastery.

You can Create Your Destiny

We, all of us, are creator beings that enrich the drama of life. Life can be viewed as a cocktail of joy and sorrow that we are forced to drink; or we can view the life as a wonder that can be created every moment we live. It is all a matter of individual perspective. An adjustment in your focus can alter your life forever. We can live as conscious choice makers creating our lives every moment of our existence.

Then why are the majority of us living their lives woven around hurt, anger, hatred, stress, tension and recrimination? It is because people do not understand and accept the fact that by changing our own thought patterns, perception and lifestyle, we can contribute towards changing the world around us. It is because people fail to take responsibility of their own lives.

The 'karma' theory has done more disservice than service, due to wrong understanding about it. People often blame their fates for anything happening to them and others, while many misfortunes could be avoided by being alert and aware in life. Many moments of joy could be created if we could shape and direct the thoughts consciously. A pure and positive mind helps to erase or transcend the negative 'karma'.

What is karma, really? Well, to put it plainly, it is the collection of your past thoughts and behavioural patterns imprinted as impressions in the memory. Karma can not bind you when you live your life consciously, creating every moment of it. Karma does not stick to you as you let go of the past every moment. Karma can not enslave you when you live the life with strength, courage and determination. It can never taint the vast and limitless purity of your inner being.

An abundance of positive energy exists within and around us, waiting to be harnessed. We all have deep wellsprings of creativity eager to find an expression. Life is a wonderful piece of art. Be creative, as much as you can, in creating it. Approach the life with a fresh perspective. It is your life. You have the freedom to create it, decorate it with love, compassion, joy and laughter, or mar it with brooding, blaming, anger and hatred. When you live your life creatively, you are automatically connected to the source.

From Matter to Spirit: A Shift

There are different levels to our existence. Man can be either the matter, or the spirit. Just a shift in the perspective can transform your being from the material to a spiritual one. Depending on the level where your consciousness abides, you can be matter, mind, witnessing consciousness, or one with the God at the highest rung of evolution. When you think, 'I am this body', that is, when you identify with the body, mind or thoughts, you become aligned with matter. You become the matter. When you think, 'I am happy, sad, angry etc.', you are aligning yourself with the thoughts and emotions of the mind and therefore, you are the mind. When you witness and feel, 'I am the witness to everything that is happening within and around this body and mind', you are the spirit, the energy of consciousness that enlivens this body.

At a higher state of consciousness when, you know and feel yourself to be the one, indivisible and spacious cosmic consciousness, within which all the phenomena are unfolding, you have aligned yourself with God. Then you become a godly being. Then a time may come, when, you intrinsically realize that even this 'I am', the idea of knowing-being too, is external to the essence of your reality, which is the clear sky of self-revealing aware silence.

Training the Mind

Most of the seeds of our thoughts are unknowingly collected from the environment, from people we love or admire, and also from the people, we dislike. These seeds form much of the habitual and compulsive pattern of thinking going on in our mind. If the mind is too much clouded with thoughts and emotions of negative nature, it will be restless. When the mind is restless, it will be almost impossible for you to observe the thoughts, much less dissociate from them. Training of the mind is necessary to make it calm, quiet and devoid of negative conditionings of the past.

When you grow the ability to witness your thoughts, only then, you have the ability to remain rooted in the centre of your being, choosing only the thoughts of love, life, abundance and good will. If you can do that, your life will flow with effortless ease, and all auspiciousness will surround you from everywhere. We need to train the mind if we want to come out of the rigid patterns of negative conditionings. A well-trained mind can be your best friend to serve you the highest good. A well-trained mind is in service of the inner Guru. When the mind is trained to cherish only the thoughts that are beneficial to you and others, it will retain its calmness and composure in all situations. The surface of the lake of mind will be tranquil and the inner light will shine bright through it. Consequently, it will be almost effortless for you to connect to the source, to the inner light shining within.

Lessons in Training the Mind

Many seekers try to control the mind, or fight it in an effort to master it. That is a sure recipe for failure. Mind is not your enemy, and there is a reason why it behaves in a certain way. You need to know the reason. The mind needs to be dealt with great caution, sensitivity, patience, resilience, intelligence and determination.

Since thoughts are ideas and imaginations, they can be replaced, changed or transformed, if we are conscious about them. The mind can be trained to accept or reject something. The training may be conscious or unconscious, though. The mind is unconsciously trained by our experiences and exposures to events, situations and persons. When our mind is trained, it reacts in a certain way to external stimulus. It learns to interpret the things, persons and situations in a certain way. When the mind is trained to accept something, the mind interprets it as 'Good'. When the mind is trained to reject something, it interprets the thing as 'Bad'. Then, there are things to which the mind is neutral. An example of how the mind can be trained to treat things as good, bad or neutral, is habits such as smoking. The first time one inhales the smoke is definitely not very pleasant to the senses. However, over the time the mind is so much trained to accept it as good and desirable personality trait, that it might be very difficult to quit the habit.

A properly trained mind can be your best friend, to steer you smoothly towards the source of fulfilment, just as an untrained mind, or a mind trained with unhealthy habits can create havoc in the life. So often, we unconsciously train the mind with unhealthy habits of anger, hatred, worry or fear that make us experience sorrow now, and also, in the future. Everybody will vouchsafe for the fact that experiencing thoughts of anger or fear is not a pleasant experience. It is a sorrowful state of consciousness; it generates further sorrow in the future.

If you can remember the truth of oneness of all life and the pristine purity of consciousness as your inner Guru, it helps to cure the unwholesome thoughts. Train the mind consciously to think of good and auspicious thoughts that serves the best interests of you, bringing happiness now, and also, in the future. There are three main points to remember in training the mind.

First, the thoughts and emotions that you experience are, really, not yours, as you normally believe them to be. They happen to you. Sometimes the mind produces them as original; sometimes it brings them up from its repository; and sometimes it simply gathers them from the environment.

Second, thoughts and ideas are not absolute truths. They are just beliefs; the mind believes them to be true, which may not be the case in reality. The idea, the mind cherishes, are proved wrong very often.

Third, you have a choice regarding your thoughts and emotions, though they seem to be automatic due to long unconsciousness. Thoughts can be accepted or rejected, replaced or transformed, only if we are conscious of the thought, if we are conscious of our choice to accept or reject them.

Many techniques are used for training the mind. We divide them in to two categories. The first is to eliminate the negative thoughts and the second is to keep the mind focussed on the positive, life-oriented virtues.

Guide Your Thoughts

To train the mind you need to be conscious of your thoughts. Choose your thoughts wisely, as a gardener will choose the species of plants and flowers to decorate his garden. Create the garden of your being by wisely choosing your thoughts.

Never allow an unwholesome thought to stay with you. You need to examine honestly the contents of your mind. Pay particular attention to any thought or emotion that repeats itself. Make it a habit of listening to the chatter of your mind, by asking yourself often, "What am I thinking now? Is this thought beneficial for me, or for people near or dear to me? Will it not harm anybody?" If you find the thought harmful for anybody, summarily reject that thought for your own good. Welcome only those wholesome thoughts that will serve good to you and others.

Replace One Thought by Another

Thoughts are energy vibrations. They can not be destroyed because energy can not be destroyed. However, they can be transformed. This is a practice given by the ancient sage Patanjali, and later prescribed by the Buddha. This technique is based on the basic rule that the mind can not hold on to two thoughts in a single point of time; hence, the unwholesome thoughts can be eliminated by purposefully bringing in another thought of contrary nature.

Like anything in this universe, thoughts too are in a state of constant change. Thoughts alter in a split moment, giving us the false impression that we are thinking more than one thought at a time. The obsessive thoughts come back repeatedly, giving us the false impression that one single thought is continuing for a long time without a gap. When we know the truth of gap existing between the thoughts, and when we are aware of our power to choose, we can easily replace one thought with another.

Like thoughts, emotions too can be replaced. You can replace a negative emotion by a positive one. Emotions can easily be transformed when they are replaced by emotions of opposite nature. For example, when you are angry, you may choose to bring the thought of forgiveness by remembering how the person, you are angry with, loved or served you earlier. You may think about how nice a relationship once both of you used to share. Or else, you may try to think of someone you really love, or someone who loves you. If you can do that, you will find that the energy of anger within you is rapidly transformed to energy of a different nature.

When you are overcome with fear, think of the divine protection of your inner Guru as a soothing and protective light surrounding you. Guilt too can be replaced by the thought of the light of love and forgiveness of your inner guru that envelops you within its orb. Love can replace all negative emotions. Replace fear with love. Replace anger, hatred and guilt with love. The thought of the loving light of your inner Guru heals you from within.

However, if you find some obstinate thought coming back repeatedly, do not pay much attention to it and be aloof to it as you do for an unwanted guest. Then bring in to your mind some wholesome, positive thought. You may bring it from a pleasant memory, you may like to read an inspirational passage from the book you like, or, you may pay your attention to a wonderful prayer of goodwill that uplifts the mind. Alternatively, you may simply divert your attention to some job at hand.

The clue is the knowledge that, a thought perishes, if you do not pay your attention to it. Thoughts are impermanent in nature, like anything in this existence. Hence, when you manage to hold your attention to somewhere else, ignoring an unwanted thought, it perishes. Be intelligent and creative in choosing contrary thoughts to replace a negative one.

Use Affirmations

Affirmations have been very popular these days. Believing in what you say and repeating it with feeling is the key to success in working with affirmations. They can be powerful tool to inject positive ideas and thought patterns in your mind. Thus, over the time, the old habitual pattern of self-destructive negative thought patterns give way to these fresh positive thoughts.

Our physical and mental beings are made of accumulated thoughts. Thoughts accumulated and repeated over time makes a pattern, and ultimately manifests as our physical and mental being to be experienced in our consciousness. It is the thoughts that manifests as external circumstances. Here comes the importance of developing and culturing positive and benevolent thought patterns. They can be used to remake your being and circumstances by destroying the old patterns. Affirmations are wonderful tools for that. You may create small positive statements to affirm during specific hours of the day, or in specific situations.

Develop positive self-dialogues during a trial or in an adverse situation. These are the times when most people unconsciously cultivate negative inner dialogue, thus aggravating the situation. Remember, if you believe and say to yourself that you will overcome, you will really be able to overcome, however trying or difficult the situation might be.

Whenever you catch yourself having a negative inner dialogue, change it to a positive one, or replace it with a constructive one. For example, if you catch your mind saying, 'So many bad omens; this is going to be a bad day', immediately change it to 'Mind knows nothing; everything is going to happen in my favour today.' If you catch your mind saying, 'I can not possibly be successful in this job', immediately change it to 'I choose to be successful; hence, I will be successful by the grace of my inner Guru'. Know that, as the consciousness you are the choice maker, while as a body-mind you are not.

If you notice doubts peeping in your mind, brush it aside with a 'mind knows nothing' attitude. Then, silently affirm the positive statements a few times, with faith and feeling. Do not believe your mind when it says negative. It really knows very little of what the power of Grace can accomplish. Infinite is the power and potential of our inner Guru whose nature is pure consciousness. It is always ready to serve you so long as you are at its service. By cultivating a positive attitude and positive inner dialogue, you serve it the best.

In many religious cultures, people practice the habit of chanting a mantra. Mantras are nothing but affirmations of divine nature. They remind us of the divinity within us. Nevertheless, one should take care in chanting a mantra. Mindless chanting can make one unaware, instead of creating awareness of the divine.

Choose Peace and Harmony

Learning to choose peace and harmony is every situation is the key to having them in your life. As we discussed earlier, at every step and every moment in life we make choices, mostly unconsciously. An untrained and unconscious mind chooses discord, disharmony and war to its own detriment. Hence, train the mind to choose harmony, peace, accord and balance in everything and every situation. Choose harmony, when you interact with people. Learn to disagree without hatred and rancour. Be friendly and live in harmony with the earth and the environment, the plants and the animals. Take care not to disturb the peace of any being and you will be automatically choosing peace and harmony in your life.

Learn to Love and Accept Yourself

Learn to love and accept yourself, your body, mind and being in its totality. Though this may sound obvious, very few people truly love themselves and act upon on their interest. Loving yourself is the beginning of the journey that ends in loving others, and endless happiness follows as a result.

Accept yourself with all your strengths and faults, as a loving mother accepts her child with care and concern. Even if the child is difficult, she accepts her child totally and still works for its improvement, for its benefit. Forgive yourself when you fail to live up to your expectation. It does not mean that you do not try to improve. However, admonishing yourself does not serve anything other than self-defeat and self-alienation. You can improve only when you have accepted yourself so totally that your mind and body becomes one integrated being, and nothing is hidden in the backyard of your mind. Now you are able to watch negative thoughts, feelings, habits or traits with certain detachment and you are free to take corrective steps. It is necessary to befriend the mind because mind is a helpful companion what gives you the necessary impetus at the beginning of your journey towards the core of your being.

When you accept yourself totally, with all your strengths and weaknesses, you will also be able to accept others as they are. To demand others to be different from as they are, amounts to arrogance meaning to dictate life for that person and infringing upon their freedom. Everybody is a unique creation of consciousness; consequently, all should have the freedom to be what they are, so long as they are not harming others. Learning to accept yourself as well as others as they are, would bring much peace, tranquillity and happiness to you.

Unfortunately, difficult times can make us feel unworthy, or forgotten by the world. Do not fail to love and respect yourself at such times. Remember that we are as worthy, whole and loved by the Divine on the rough roads as on the smooth.

Appreciate the Beauty of Life in Trivia

We should learn to appreciate the inherent beauty of life that peeps as much through the graceful smile of a wrinkled old face as through the innocent smile of a baby. Everywhere and in everything the beauty and wonder of consciousness is peeping through. As we grow old, we forget to get in touch with that. We forget to appreciate the beauty hidden in a piece of wood or a lump of clay, with which a child may play for hours. The mind needs to be consciously trained to reclaim the lost paradise of the childhood, to learn to wonder just about anything.

You can do that by consciously paying attention to the little joys of having a healthy body, being able to breathe the fresh air, walking on the grass, having a cup of tea, relaxing and enjoying a soothing music and the like. These little joys are very easily available to most of us but our minds are normally trained to be neutral to these experiences or ignore them. We are often caught in the habit of taking things and people for granted.

The mind remains caught in the net of thinking, and takes note of these seemingly 'trivial' experiences, only when it feels a lack. For example, we are aware of what a blessings a healthy body is, when we are sick. We are aware of the bliss that breathing offers only when we have caught cold and have a blocked nose. Thus, the normal, unconscious training of the mind is only to take note of the lacks. It is understandable why boredom and unhappiness is so widespread, even among those that have apparently everything required for a happy living.

For living our lives joyfully, we need to teach our minds to enjoy small things. From time to time, remind yourself to have a notice of the small things happening around you and amuse yourself with that. Remind yourself often not to take life too seriously. Sincerity and seriousness is not the same thing. Sincerity adds integrity and dignity to our character, while too much seriousness robs us of the ability to laugh, enjoy and smile at the funny side of life.

Learn to laugh and giggle. We may learn that from the children. They have the unique gift of spontaneously living in the moment and having fun in just about any situation. Form a habit to see beauty and wonder in everything and everybody, including you. This habit will completely wipe away the negative conditionings of the past and make your mind lighter and happier. Enjoy making fun about yourself. Goal oriented persons are seldom happy in life. They set one goal after another and with their mind set only on the goal, they often forget to enjoy what life offers on the way, and in the process miss the life totally. Learn to enjoy the way as much as you would enjoy when you reach the destination.

Focus on the Bliss Within

This practice reminds the mind that happiness comes from within rather than from some external objects, as it usually believes. As far as our mind is concerned, it needs to be trained to be happy. This may happen when you learn to love and accept yourself. You learn to accept your fellow beings as they are, and not as they should be, according to your mental interpretations. You learn to accept and enjoy life as it unfolds, and do not impose conditions on it. For this, you need to take time, to be quiet, to appreciate the beauty in life.

Before we further elaborate on these points, let us see what happiness really is. As we pointed out earlier, all the experiences happen within your consciousness. The experience of happiness is no exception. Nothing can make you happy, if you do not allow happiness to happen within your being. Since everybody is unique so far, as body and mind and social standard are concerned, we have no universal recipe for happiness. What makes one happy may not bring happiness to another. For example, a rich and spicy dinner may bring happiness to someone used to such food, while it may not be even agreeable to someone used to a different food habit. If you are an artist, finishing a nice piece of painting may bring you such happiness as no material thing can offer.

Having good foods, a great job, a nice house, a nice car and a kind mate are socially accepted norms for a happy living. However, if these things would buy happiness then the persons having these things would always be in a happy state of mind. The probability would be that the richest persons would be the happiest in the world. However, we all know that the fact is often contrary. Happiness is never a thing that money, relationship or any other material things can buy. Moreover, happiness is a very fleeting sensation, which often slips out of hand in this temporal world where everything is in constant change.

If you live with an open eye, you will seldom find a happy person. You might have all the things to be happy, judged by material and social standards, but still be very unhappy. A loss in the share market may make you unhappy. A stray comment from an office colleague can mar your day, making you unhappy. A remark from a neighbour may make you feel miserable. If you are at the mercy of others, things and people, to make you happy, then, happiness will elude you forever. Teach your mind that if your happiness depends on things outside of your being, like a thing, a person or a situation, this means slavery to these external conditions. A slave seldom gets happiness. In that case, unhappiness would be a constant shadow following your happiness.

What most of us do not know is that happiness is the natural state of our being. It is something happening within our consciousness. It does not solely depend on the external conditions. You can find happiness from the external objects and people, so long as you are aware of their impermanence, so long as you are prepared to let them go, if required, and remain happy within your own being. Loving yourself is the key to finding happiness within your being.

The quest for happiness is a fine trick of our unconscious nature to fool us. If you spend some time reflecting on the behaviour of your own mind, you may be surprised by what you discover. You will find that happiness is something that is always available to us. A thing or a person you love makes you happy because your attention gets absorbed in to that and this absorption silences the random dialogues in your mind, albeit momentarily. Hence, the natural happiness of your being surfaces up to make you feel happy. When the fresh charm of the thing or the person wears away and you take them for granted, the same thing or person looses the ability to absorb your mind. As a result, the random thoughts are activated again in your mind, and the light of happiness fades away under the cloud of thoughts.

The same thing is true when something you do makes you happy. When you are doing something you enjoy, your attention is totally absorbed in it and thoughts lessen or disappear altogether depending on the degree of absorption. The feelings of happiness surfaces and pervades your being, as a result. So, the conclusion is, your mind needs to do nothing for making you happy. The job of mind is to produce thoughts, most of which make you unhappy. Just think of a situation when your mind produces a torrent of thoughts; if the thoughts are negative in nature, such as those of anger or hatred, you become miserable. If the thoughts are random in nature, you feel bored or restless. Unhappiness or boredom can be 'created', by a flurry thoughts, whereas, happiness is a state of few or no thoughts. Lesser the thoughts, greater the happiness you feel.

As your mind becomes more and more subtle, you will find it easy to tune with the inner melody of bliss that flows within like a stream buried under the sands. Keep your focus on that unborn, undying bliss. Any external cause of happiness only unravels or manifests only a part of that inner sky of bliss.

Our unconscious nature often tries to overshadow and crush our all-powerful Self, by producing shadows of fear, anxiety, sadness, gloom and monotony. Throw them away immediately, as soon as you become aware of them. Throw out from your mind anything and anybody that makes you miserable or unhappy. Train the mind not to cherish or cultivate unhappy thoughts and cultivate happy thoughts. Find out any reason to be happy in an existing situation.

Consciously find what makes you happy without clouding your consciousness and focus on that.

The key to maintain the glimpse of the inner stream of happiness is to keep your focus on the inner feeling of joy in any joyful situation of life. Be it listening to your favourite music, painting, gardening, or writing, singing, or just walking, anything that keeps you in a light spirit will do. Do what you love to do. Be where you love to be. Only thing is to keep your focus on the joy that flows from within, and not on the object outside. In doing so, we need to be alert that the joy of the present moment must not adversely affect the body and mind in the future. Eternal and limitless bliss is our inner Guru and it never contradicts the body or the mind. If the present moment of joy brings bodily and mental suffering in the future, then the joy is not wholesome in nature and it is not worth having. We need to use discretion and awareness in choosing our source of bliss. Living in this way, gradually, you will be able to feel happiness just for no reason at all.

All of us are allotted with a limited span of time in this human body. The time will be over, anyway, whether you choose to live it brooding, fretting and fuming, or you choose to take on the life on your terms by resolving to remain blissful, come what may. However daunting the circumstances may be, refuse to succumb before it. Learn to ignore it and remain blissful with whatever, you find, makes you happy. If you can do that, you will find that the unconscious nature is forced to bow down before the all-powerful Self, by presenting you more and more favourable circumstances in course of time.

If you remain blissful, your heart will be filled with gratitude towards the source of bliss. You will feel blessed and everything will fall in to place. When we are blissful, our luminous Self-nature peeps through the curtain of this inert physical body. This is the reason, why a blissful countenance attracts people. A blissful consciousness is ever aligned with its essence; hence, it attracts abundance, fortune and all good things on earth. When you are blissful, you emit energy of very sublime nature that never goes with darkness, disharmony, misfortune, disease, sadness or poverty. All these things will go away from you. This one practice can evolve you beyond your imagination. This one practice may awaken the inner Guru, if pursued diligently, consciously and continuously. If you can pursue this single practice under all conditions of life, you do not need to do anything else.

Practice of Letting Go and Accepting Changes

Letting go is an important lesson in training the mind. If we want to really relax and be happy, we need to learn to take life less seriously. We need to learn to let go. Everything is impermanent in this life. This was the first noble truth taught by the Buddha. If we can remember it often, it will help us to let go and relax. As human beings we are often hooked in the habit of clinging to things, people, thoughts or an existing situation or circumstances, be it good or bad. We do this because changes make us feel insecure or uncomfortable. In wanting things to remain the same, people often cling to their misery. Letting go is the most important lesson that life can teach us.

Let go of everything and everyone that pulls you backward towards the past. Let go of the unnecessary past, of fixed ideas. Let go of the negative thoughts and emotions. Let go of grudges, anger and resentment. Forgive and forget so that you can move on with your life. This will give you tremendous freedom. If you can do this continuously, eventually a miracle will happen. You will be able to discover the silent and peaceful centre within you. You will find that you are self-sufficient and self-illumined. You will discover the hidden spring of peace and happiness within you. The quality of your life will change forever.

Apply 'letting go' in all the areas of life and you will see that getting rid of the excess baggage of life makes life so much celebration resulting in release and freedom. While it is important to take lessons from the past, do not cling to the past. Approach the life with a fresh outlook. Be creative in responding to what life may present you. Do not let your past experiences taint the present. Every day is a new beginning. Every moment is born fresh. Every breath brings with it the promise and freedom of a new beginning.

Consciously let go of everything that does not contribute to your sense of well-being. In this way, you let go of the past. It is as easy as that. As we flow with time, we learn to embrace changes. Change is the heart of the process called life. Just look around and you will see that change is happening every day, every moment. If we do not embrace change, how can we hope to improve our lives?

Changes can be a harbinger for improvement when it is embraced in a right spirit. Even if the change is of an unwelcome nature, like losing a job, or something like that, take it as a scope for betterment in life and not as a failure. When you learn to readjust yourself happily with the change that life brings on the way, you are surely moving one-step further ahead on the path of evolution.

Even in our spiritual life, we can not evolve unless we are prepared to let go of the preconceived ideas, notions, learned doctrines or dogmas. We can not evolve if we fail to accept new experiences and insights as they come in the process of evolution. One after another, experiences will happen; insights will come as a flood, on the way. Sometimes spiritual seekers have a tendency to cling to experiences and insights; but, if you do that, it will only pull you back. Always be in an attitude of 'let go'. Ultimate spiritual enlightenment is not a state of knowing; it is a state of being. Sometimes seekers stop on the midway, and hold on to some dogmatic idea that came during some meditative absorption. Letting go, being open and adjusting happily to the changes is the most sublime lesson to learn on the path.

Dealing with Negative Emotions

Spiritual seekers are often troubled with thoughts and emotions of unwholesome nature. This is a great hindrance for spiritual development and well-being of the seeker. Negative or unwholesome thoughts produce a veil covering the inner light, while wholesome thoughts brighten it. It is important to realize that all negative mental states such as depression, hopelessness, fear, jealously, lust or greed are disempowering. They arise out of the false belief that one's wellbeing and fulfilment lies outside of oneself.

Negative thoughts like jealousy or anger hurt the source more than that object it is directed to. Remember that we can not harm others, even by thoughts, without first harming ourselves. Negative thoughts make one unconscious. We should take care to fill our mind with the thoughts of peace, harmony and good will.

Whenever you catch yourself having a negative inner dialogue, change it to a positive one, or replace it with a constructive one. Do not be discouraged or frustrated if you are not successful at the first instance. Remember that, frustration too is a thought. You will be successful if you persevere.

The thoughts that carry negative emotions with them, like anger, worry, hatred, jealousy or fear, store huge energy within them. If they are not released or transformed, they could destroy the body by generating toxic chemicals, which, if stored in the body, is capable to create diseases. We are going to discuss some simple practices that come handy to deal with the negative emotions. See for yourself which technique suits you better. However, though the techniques can prove to be effective, you will get rid of all unhealthy states permanently only when you deeply realize that we ourselves are the true sources of our happiness.

Breathe out Negative Thoughts

This simple but powerful practice can prove extremely helpful at the time of distress when negative emotions like anger or fear ravages the mind. Take a deep breath and as you breathe out, feel that you release the negative emotion with the long outgoing breath. Repeat the process, with your attention focussed on the outgoing breath. Within a short time, you will feel much relief.

Be Mindful of the Sensations Inside

This practice is a corollary to the practice discussed above. While you breathe out, put your attention on the feelings and sensations inside your body. Do not resist the feeling as it arise. Allow yourself to become aware of the sense of space that surrounds and permeates this feeling-sensation. Notice this feeling inside the body from the space outside of it. Now allow yourself to sink into the root of the feeling. Did the feeling dissipate in the field of spacious awareness?

Now begin a journey of awareness. Begin from your throat, then move to your heart, and then, gradually move to the lower abdomen. As you gently breathe out, be intensely aware of the sensations produced in your throat. Then breathe in and move downwards to your heart as you breathe out. Continue to breathe in and out, until you feel that the heaviness or numbness in your heart has softened or disappeared. Then again, breathe in and as you breathe out, check the centre approximately two inches below the navel.

When all the sensations are gone, the unhealthy thought and the corresponding feeling of hurt will disappear too. As you keep focussing your awareness on the sensations inside your body, the negative emotions disappear just as the clouds disappear in the presence of the Sun. You will be surprised to notice that, the knots and hurtful feelings born out of the negative emotions dissolve, as the sensations inside your body disappear.

Breathe Through the Lower Abdomen

When powerful emotions storm the mind, bring the mind back to its home. There is a centre situated near the navel, approximately two inches below it. This is the place where the mind can be grounded and protected from the storm of emotions. When unwholesome emotions appear, slowly, breathe in and out through this point, keeping your awareness anchored in your breaths. Within a short time, you will feel calm and grounded.

Look at it Without Resistance

Looking at an emotion deeply without resistance and judgement helps to unknot and release a deep-seated negative emotion. If there is a fear, can you allow yourself to look at it without resistance? Can you come to peace with it? Once you look at the emotion and accept the very worst that can happen through it, you come to peace with it. Once you live an emotion deeply in perfect awareness, the emotion, fear in this case, loses its power over you. Ask yourself, what is the worst possible thing that could happen? Allow yourself to experience the worst possible scenario with full awareness. Come to peace with it by accepting the imagined situation. Allow yourself to live it fully in your mind with perfect awareness about how you feel when living it. Take note of every bit of all possible feelings and sensations that you may go through by living it mentally. When you have lived it fully you will find that the emotion have lost its hold on you. Now you can release the emotion with breath, by taking slow, deep breaths. If you have the courage to stay with it long enough, you will find that the fear (any unhealthy emotion, for that matter) eventually dissipates and ultimately, it is completely released. The light of your awareness melts the block of ignorance that fear, or any negative emotion is. If you are once successful in doing that, then the growing sense of ease and wellbeing will make you more and more willing to face your deepest issues and you will soon find yourself gratefully releasing every negative and unhealthy emotion easily and effortlessly.

Practicing Virtues

Practice forgiveness, patience, generosity, respect and gratitude towards yourself and others. It is a sure way to attract abundance and fulfilment from the reservoir of Life. The grace of inner Guru manifests as the harmonious conditions, peaceful environment and the best of everything that comes to you. The practice of the five golden virtues of the heart will make your inner sky clear and cloudless and the inner light will shine bright. A forgiving heart never suffers from depression. A person of patience is blessed with the clarity and joy of a serene heart. A generous person will find plenty of reasons to be happy about. A person who is respectful towards others will find many friends around her. A grateful heart is seldom sad. In the mysterious world of mind, the effects produce the causes, just as in the external world causes produce the effect. Practiced in the light of this understanding, the following virtues would lighten the heart, remove the veil of darkness and reveal the inner Sun.

Though religions down the ages have glorified these virtues, we should never practice them as doctrines, maxims or dogma thrust upon by some external authority. If we did that it would further cloud the consciousness; if we have rigid insistence of 'should and should not' about practising these virtues, they will seem like burden that makes life heavy, instead of lightening it. See for yourself if practising these virtues adds to your inner clarity, peace and joy. See, how you feel when you practice them. Then, you will find enough inspiration to pursue these practices.

Forgiveness Liberates

Forgiveness is a divine virtue. It makes you divine. To be able to forgive others, first you should learn to forgive yourself for anything that you regret doing. Learning to forgive yourself is the first step in learning to forgive others. Let go of the memory of the things, persons and situations that brought pain, and never look back.

Forgiveness lightens the heart by releasing us from the chain of anguish and anger. Forgiveness is an important exercise in letting go of the past. Mind has a tendency to hold on to the memory of past hurt. It runs the film of past events, and in the process, clouds the consciousness. Understand that the past has totally ended. Remembering and reliving them in your mind will serve no purpose other than hurting yourself further. When we consciously let go of the past, we lighten the burden of life.

By releasing the past, you walk towards a new beginning, opening the doors for better things to happen to you. This way, you are not doing a favour to others; rather you are doing favour to yourself by stepping out of the chain of suffering. Holding on to any hurtful feelings does more damage to you than it does to anyone else. By forgiving, or letting go, huge amount of energy so long blocked as anger, hatred or revengeful thoughts will be released and transformed. The released energy will flow in the body, heal the body and brighten up the mind. This creates happiness.

We should consciously release the hurtful baggage of the past. Know that, it is our choice to carry on the baggage or put it down forever. Be the wise choice maker that you are. You will find that conscious choice to forgive, let go and move on with your life will be such a liberating experience for you.

Patience Empowers You with Clarity

Patience is the golden rule for an alert and peaceful life. It brings serenity within us. It can turn every situation in our favour. Patience gives us clarity and peace. Patience makes room for making the right choice, at the right moment. It makes you the master of the Nature, where everything is in a constant flux.

When you are not in a hurry, you automatically retain your composure and clarity. In certain situations in life, it is better to wait and see rather than rushing with thoughtless speech and hasty action. If you wait for a moment before opening your mouth, you will have fewer occasions to regret what you said. Patience is the cornerstone for building a good relationship in the home and in the workplace.

In a queue in the post office or the bank, in the store, or during the traffic jam, we can take the opportunity to practice patience. These are times when we are forced to be with ourselves. Being angry, frustrated or irritated, blaming others or the situation can serve nothing other than raising your blood pressure and stress level. We do not need extraordinary intelligence to understand this. Yet, that is what most of us do, when faced with such a situation. Our mind reacts with irritation, anger, or frustration, as if, by fretting and fuming it can change the situation. Next time whenever you catch yourself losing patience, smile and be on alert. Practice of patience can create a grace and serenity in our being.

Generosity Illumines the Heart

The word generosity can be used to mean kindness, open-heartedness, charity and bounty. Here we are using the word in every possible sense of the term. Try to be generous to someone and notice how you feel inside yourself. Every time we are generous, unfailingly we feel good because generosity opens the heart centre and connects us with the inner Guru. Generosity also attracts abundance. We are here on earth to love and care, to give and share. A stingy person can never be truly happy; can never find real joy and fulfilment in life. We should make it a habit to share with others what we have. Generosity does not necessarily require you to spend money for others. Generosity also means being nice and kind to someone. You do not need to spend a penny for that. You can be generous when you praise someone for a worthy cause.

Respect Brings Wisdom and Greatness

Respect unlocks your hidden potential for wisdom and greatness. Respects to one's own self and respect for others is the recipe for greatness. Always treat others with respect. Even the children deserve to be treated respectfully. This we, the grownups often forget. Every soul has come on this planet with a purpose and everyone, however fallen, carries the signature of divinity within, though they might have apparently strayed from the path.

Our inner Guru is the Guru of all, and abides in every heart. When you have respect for everybody, as you have for yourself, you will grow in wisdom. You will eventually realize that in plants, animals and even in the insentient things, the same divine glow sparks, though unnoticed by the eyes of flesh. Cherish in your heart respect for everyone and treat others with respect. You will be astonished to find that you will be rewarded back with the same, even from the most unexpected sources.

Gratitude Brings Auspiciousness

The last but not the least is, remember to be grateful. Gratitude is essential to attract abundance in our lives. Gratitude is necessary because the whole universe is an interconnected web of interdependence. Every moment of our being, we are receiving from this universe. Every breath of us is borrowed from the atmosphere, from the trees that recycle the carbon dioxide to the life-giving oxygen. All the food we take in is borrowed from the earth, from the plants and animals on the planet. We could not survive, if the Sun would not caress us with warmth and energy. What would we have to drink if the rivers and streams would not provide us with pure water?

The artificial life in the city has taught us to be so arrogant and ungrateful, that we completely forget about our dependent existence. We forget that, we survive by being on the receiving end, every moment of our lives. We have forgotten to be grateful. How much grateful we are to the person who gives or lends us something we need? Our entire existence as a human being is a borrowed existence. Should we not become eternally grateful to the Sun, the earth, the plants, animals, rivers and other human beings on the planet who made our existence possible? To live with a grateful heart is the way of conscious and enlightened living.

Gratitude should be the essential norm and ethics of our life. It can change our lives in a profound and miraculous way.

Meister Eckhart, a German mystic used to say, "If the only prayer you say in your whole life is, 'Thank you,' that would suffice. We should be grateful for every moment of innocent joys that life presents to us. We should be thankful for every breath, and every sign of beauty and wonder. Gratitude is another name of Self-love. By being grateful to life and people, you are really being grateful to your Self.

We usually have many moments of innocent joys of living. Be grateful for that. When we live mindfully, we learn to be grateful for small things, like, a well-cooked bowl of food served with love and care, for an understanding co-worker, for a loving friend or relative. We learn to be grateful for all the generous and good people in our lives. Life brings so many blessings to us everyday, which we often take for granted. A loving and caring friend is a blessing. An understanding co-worker is a blessing. A Sunlit morning is a blessing. A silent starry night is a blessing. A healthy body is a blessing. The number is more than we can count. But how many of us acknowledge these blessings in their lives? We can make a habit to find at least one reason to be grateful to life. This simple practice can enrich lives beyond imagination. Our gratitude need not be always expressed in a loud or pronounced utterance of thankfulness. What is important is our attitude. When gratitude flows within our heart like a silent undercurrent, our lives become tremendously rich.

Practice the Virtues to Open the Mind

The most important understanding behind these practices is that, we practice these virtues not for the sake of others, but for the sake of our own happiness. We practice them to open the bud of our mind to make it blossom as a flower. However, people around us are also benefited along with ourselves, when we practice the virtues. These are seeds of happiness, that when watered with conscious attention, will manifest as trees bearing the fruits of joy, love and peace in abundance.

We practice these qualities not only towards other fellow beings, but also towards ourselves. If you can not forgive yourself, you can not forgive others. If you do not have respect for yourself, you can not possibly treat others with respect. If you are not generous to yourself, you can not be generous to others. If you do not practice these virtues to yourself, then even if you try to practice them for others, they will not come from your heart; they will not be genuine. These are divine virtues. Culturing these virtues will unleash the divine power latent within you.

Practising Conscious Choice

The Divine is playing in this very body and mind of yours wearing the veil of forgetfulness. We can make this play conscious, or we can play it in the absolute darkness of unconsciousness; it all depends on you. When you are reacting in an unconscious manner to the people and situations in your life, the play remains unconscious. When you act and respond to life in a conscious manner, as a conscious choice-maker, the play is made conscious. It depends on the degree of your awareness and alignment with the Divine within you as your inner Guru. Self-power is the power of God.

The practices, we have discussed above, can be pursued unconsciously, as some tenets to be followed; or they can be practiced as a conscious choice to manifest the Divine within you. Conscious intention, conscious decision and conscious effort, these three are very important, whether you want success in your practice, in your life or in your spiritual search.

Conscious Intention

Wishes and desires are something common to all the mortals on earth; but more often than not, they are buried under the unconscious layers of the mind. This is true for all material and spiritual searches. Even in your spiritual search, you have a desire, desire for peace, God, Self-realization, Moksha or Nirvana, that propels you to undertake some practices.

Conscious intention is very uncommon, though logically it seems so self-evident. What is most common in common people is wistful thinking, like, "Oh, only if I was fortunate enough to have such and such thing", or, "I don't know whether, or when I am going to get that". This type of mental dialogue shows the absence of a conscious choice to have the thing you want. Conscious intention means, you know what you want. You know where you are going. You say to yourself, "I know, I want this". Conscious intention is the beginning of any successful endeavour.

Conscious Decision

Next step is making conscious decision. You decide that you deserve to have the thing you wanted. You believe that even now you are capable of having that. This is reflected by thoughts such as, "I deserve that. I am going to have that"; or, "I choose and decide to have that", or "I'll have that". This second phase is very important. Unless, you yourself believe that you deserve the thing you want, who will? Unless you decide for yourself consciously to have the thing you want, you will be left at the mercy of somebody else to do that for you.

Conscious Effort

Once you have made conscious intention and conscious decision, the message reaches the depth of your being where powers are unleashed and the work begins for its realization. Forces begin to work in your favour. Now, you are in a position to exert conscious effort in a one-pointed and undaunted manner, to work for obtaining the aim or the object of your wish. Once you get to work, you should do it with all your strength, confidence and determination, taking everything in your advantage, whatever might be the circumstances. Allow nothing to come on your way; allow nothing to intimidate you.

These three practices of conscious choice unfold the divinity within you. They make you aligned with your inner Guru. These are essential recipe for success in all material as well as spiritual endeavour. When you practice them, all the forces on the heaven and earth will be on your side to protect and support you. This is the secret of awakening to the glory residing within you.

Chapter Six

CORE METHODS AND PRACTICES

"On this path effort never goes to waste, and there is no failure. Even a little effort toward spiritual awareness will protect you from the greatest fear."

--The Bhagavad Gita [2:40]

The Path

In spiritual journey, path and goal are the same. Really speaking, it is not a journey, at all. The 'journey', or the 'path', these are words used for linguistic convenience. In the search for your inner Guru, you do not need to go anywhere. Pure consciousness is already present pervading every cell of your being; it is present at the heart of your being as your inner Guru. The small and limited individual entity, that you believe yourself to be, is an illusory identity. It has no separate existence apart from your inner Guru, just as a character in a movie has no separate existence apart from the actor playing the role. This limited identity needs to dissolve into the oneness of the cosmic whole. Still, in a way it is not even dissolving. Your inner Guru as the pure consciousness is always full in itself. Nothing can be added to or removed from it. The light is already present. Only when you are not aware of your light, you need to make some effort.

Since our bodies and minds are unique, each person's spiritual path is also unique. In a unique way, through unique experiences in lives, you have come to this point along the path of evolution. Hence, there can not be a single prescription thrust upon everybody to follow. What can help one to grow and evolve spiritually, may prove to be a hindrance for another. In ancient times, there were masters who could see through your past, detect your natural tendency and would accordingly give you instructions to follow. Growth would be faster if the practices are compatible with one's natural tendency.

We have the famous story of a monk who joined the Order of the Buddha. He was attracted to the Buddha by the peace and serenity he radiated. He loved the way of the monks and joined the Order. However, shortly after joining the community of the monks he found himself to be in a situation of utter hopelessness. He was, as if, a total misfit to the community. He could not perform, in a satisfactory manner, any work that the monks of the community shared among themselves. Nor was he able to follow the practice of meditation that the monks followed. His mind wondered in all directions. He could not even stay on his seat of meditation. He was restless and depressed, utterly disgusted with himself, not knowing what to do with his life. Sometimes he thought that he must be in a wrong place; the meditative life of a monk was probably not for him.

Still, he felt an attraction for the Buddha and did not feel like going back to his former life. He was on the brink of despair when he was brought to the Buddha, who saw through his past lives. Buddha knew that in one of his past incarnations, this man was a jeweller per-excellence who could create excellent pieces of gold jewellery with his immaculate skill. He instructed the monk to meditate on creating a beautiful golden lotus that is symbolic of the Buddha-nature in man. The monk was overjoyed to receive such a practice from his master. He went back to his seat of meditation, and now he would found it very difficult to leave his meditation. His whole mind became completely engrossed in creating wonderful golden lotuses. Within a very short time, he developed astounding skill of concentration and progressed very fast. Meditations on the lotuses of his creation ultimately led him to the golden truth hidden within. This story illustrates the point well that, each one of us, according to his natural tendency, could follow a path to the ultimate truth, if it is rightly pointed out or known to us.

Nowadays, it is rare and difficult to find such an able personal guidance. If you do not have an able personal guidance, you need to find out for yourself which path suits you the best. There are many paths, many practices, and many methods. Not all of them will have same appeal to us because we vary in our temperaments. You may experiment on the path followed by the ancients, improvising a little here and there to suit your temperament. Out of the result of your experiments, you have to develop your own path.

In each experiment, you are going to access the same source from different directions. It will broaden your views and improve your understanding. Honesty, sincerity and perseverance are the keys. Inner peace, joy, silence, relaxation and purity are the landmarks. Trust on your inner Guru and a persistent effort will inevitably lead you towards the right path, the right practice. Once you find it, you should stick to it under all circumstances.

Many people are so much indoctrinated by a certain ideology that they make themselves closed from any teaching that does not subscribe to their ideological belief. Know for certain, that an ideology or a system of belief can never liberate you, however noble they may sound. Nothing outside of your being can liberate you. You have to walk your own path; you have to light your own lamp.

If you are honest and sincere to yourself, you will know by yourself, whether a certain path has the potential to liberate you from your fears, anxiety and restlessness. With sincere practice, putting your heart and soul in to it, you will know after a time, whether a certain path is leading you towards peace and happiness. That should be the criterion.

The Goal

The reason, why the seekers most often do not succeed in moving in to the highest realm of consciousness, is that they are trapped within their mind. They prize this intricate instrument so much that they do not wish to put it aside, even for a moment. Even the sincere spiritual aspirants become fascinated with the higher philosophies and pearls of wisdom that the mind brings up, while moving in to the higher realms of consciousness.

Being addicted to philosophies, lofty thoughts, powers and visions that mind brings up on the way, ultimately becomes impediment to the realization of our true nature. We can not really advance in spiritual life, if we do not want to move beyond the mind. Moving beyond the mind really means moving inwards, towards the inner core of our being.

The aim of the spiritual practices discussed in the subsequent sections is to dissociate from the mind. Once we are successful to observe and train the mind, we will find that our mind naturally becomes quieter and quieter, to the extent that it remains calm and tranquil for most of the time. Then it is the time to learn to dissociate from our thoughts and turn the light of our awareness within, where the inner Guru abides as the very essence of our being.

In order to dissociate from our mind, we need to keep our attention on the breath, body and posture; we need to witness the thoughts and ideas objectively, without any interpretation. Learning to detach ourselves from the continuous and compulsive chatter of the mind is the beginning of freedom. Observation of the mind makes us realize that we are not our thoughts; dissociation from the mind gives us the insight that we are not the thinker either. It gives us the glimpse of the moments when we abide as pure being, even in the total absence of the thoughts and the thinker.

When the thoughts and the thinker are absent, we feel that the awareness of our being is very open and specious, almost like the sky. It contains within it all that exists. Then we know that the Sun shining within us as the 'I Am' is the same as the one shining everywhere. Then true love blossoms within us spontaneously, to envelope the whole existence within.

The Foundation

There are some basic practices, which serve as the foundation of the spiritual life. We need to incorporate these practices as a lifestyle rather than mere practices. These simple practices form the basis on which the other practices are built up.

Learn to Release Resistances

When you undertake spiritual practices, many unconscious resistances hidden below the layers of the conscious mind may begin to surface, which may manifest as irritability, agitation or anger. The important thing to remember is that you should undertake the practices at your own pace and never overdo them. Allow your mind to take some time to adjust to your practices. If you notice severe mental agitation or physical discomfort at any stage, stop your practice for a few days and begin again with a moderate schedule. Take it light. Drink plenty of water, do some physical exercises, walk in a natural setting, and repeat with feeling several times a day, "I love this existence and I am ready to receive the benefits of my spiritual practices for the benefit of myself and for all beings in this existence." Thus, your heart centre will gradually open up and subtle resistances will dissolve.

Spiritual growth and development do not need to be arduous, as people normally believe. In fact, most of our difficulties and pain come from our unconscious resistance to growth. If we become conscious of that resistance and release it with slow, deep breaths, our growth and our path becomes easy, effortless and enjoyable.

Learning to Sit Quietly

The first and foremost practice is learning to sit quietly with yourself. This practice, though simple it may sound, may be proven the toughest to many, since the mind has long been habituated in being preoccupied with other things, people or jobs. Since the natural tendency of our mind is to fly away from ourselves, we like to keep ourselves busy with things of entertainment, people or jobs at the best. When you know how to be comfortable with yourself, with your own being, then that will be the beginning of inner freedom.

You yourself are the scientist as well as the laboratory for this inner quest. Set aside a time to be entirely with yourself. Cut off all communications with the world. Keep the mobile silenced for the time, and just sit silently with eyes closed or open. Relax within yourself. If possible, you may create your own space in your home, decorated with some beautiful paintings of landscapes. Alternatively, you may prefer to sit in close proximity to a beautiful natural setting. If your daily schedule does not permit you to do that, you may take a few minutes to be with yourself, wherever possible. You need to do nothing. Just sit silently and feel your breathing. Feel your entire body as one single unit. Feel your breath. Feel the peace of just sitting and breathing without having to do anything. Breathe deeply and in a relaxed manner. If any thought comes, do not pay attention to it. Pay attention to your breath, instead. Much tension will drop away and you will feel calmer, more focussed and clear-headed.

Maintain a Good Posture

People are very little aware of the harm they do to themselves by sitting, standing or sleeping in a bad posture. Bad posture restricts the flow of energy within the subtle channels, to create knots, obstructions or blockages in your system. This manifests as stress, imbalance and even diseases in the body and mind.

This is even more important when you start doing yoga or lead a meditative life. Much latent energy begins to awaken and flow in the subtle nerve channels that were heretofore unused. This happens not only during the meditations but also after, when you may sit, work, relax or sleep. If you have a bad posture that obstructs the flow, pain, strain, cramp or even headache may result in the body and you may experience severe swings of mood, anxiety, depression, edginess, nervousness or sleeplessness as a result. Spiritual aspirants often suffer from these symptoms without knowing the cause.

The key to a good posture is learning to keep the spine straight, but supple and relaxed. This is not something you do for half an hour or so, during your meditation, and forget when you leave the seat, as people normally believe. Learning to maintain a good posture is the first prerequisite to have a fit body and a serene and stable mind, which are not only conducive to meditation but also indispensable for a happy life. Always be aware of your posture as you sit or work, walk or lie down in the bed. Do not strain your back in any way. This is a habit worth learning through constant practice. Eventually, you will be able to be aware of your posture even when you sleep.

Learn to Observe the Sensations

Body is the temple in which God is enshrined as your inner Guru. You are a living shrine. You must enter the temple if you want to have the vision of the deity, or worship it. Entering the temple means being mindful of the energy playing in your body to manifest as sensations. God manifesting as the energy in the body can be a door to the silence of pure consciousness.

Awareness of the subtle vibrations of energy in the body opens the door to pure consciousness. So much activity is constantly going on in every one of the hundred trillion cells of our body. All the physiological functions of the body manifest as gross or subtle sensations in different parts of the body. On the mental level too, any thought or emotion produces a corresponding reaction and subsequent sensation in the body. For example, an anxious, angry or fearful thought manifests as increased heartbeat, increased flow of blood in the blood vessels, and many other reactions that produces certain sensations in different parts of the body.

Ordinarily, we have very limited awareness of the bodily sensations because most of the time, we are lost in our mental world of thoughts and emotions. Feeling your body means remaining aware of the entire tactile presence of the body as a whole, with all the sensations present within it. If you can do that, if you are grounded in the awareness of the body as an assembly of flowing sensations, it will radically change the quality of your consciousness. It will give you a glimpse of the thought-free, empty nature of your consciousness.

Scanning the body from top to the bottom is an excellent practice for keeping the awareness grounded in the body. You can do that by moving your awareness through your body from the top of your head all the way down to your feet, noticing any tense areas where the energy might be blocked, and imagining them dissolving into nothingness.

Breathing can be used as a tool to ground the awareness in the body. You may just breathe through the tense parts of your body, until the tension (or the pain) is gone. Awareness of the postures of your body can also be used for this purpose. Be aware of your postures, whenever you sit, walk or lie down. Energy follows attention, and as we bring our awareness into our body, its energy pattern and resonance begins to change. If you continue with this practice, you will be surprised. You will find that the body, which you have experienced as gross matter, is teeming with subtle currents of energy, which is often felt as light.

Use of Visualization Techniques

Visualization has a wonderful role in yoga practice. Visualization happens at the deeper level of mind than that which produces thoughts, though normally, every thought has a visual counterpart to it. Visualization happens at the "*Pashyanti*" state, described in chapter four. At this state, the thoughts exists as subtlest sound vibrations and so, they are most effectively imprinted on your subconscious mind, to bring the desired outcome faster. Visualization can help you to have a healthy body. Visualization can help you develop good concentration. Visualization can help you to have anything you want or do not want, depending on how you are using this technique, consciously or unconsciously.

Visualization can be an important practice to help you awaken the inner Guru.

Whether you believe you can visualize well or not, it is a technique, which we all use most of the time, though unconsciously. For example, when I say, 'You can practice it on your bed, just as you wake-up in the morning', does not the thought of your bedroom come to your mind as a mental picture? It surely does. As soon as you read these words, immediately you visualize your own bedroom in your mind, without least effort. Therefore, visualization as a practice is deceptively simple, and effective, nevertheless.

Your senses already know how to visualize and respond well to it. For example, if I ask you to visualize an orange in your hand and then I ask you to visualize yourself peeling it, smelling it and having a bite of it, most likely, your tongue will salivate in reality, though there is no real orange. So, your body reacts to visualization as if it were a real thing. Body is deeply linked to mind at the subconscious level. Thus, visualization can go a long way to control the mind or to imprint desirable ideas on the deeper level of the mind, preparing the ground for its manifestation.

Positive visualization can remove the blockages of the subtle channels in the nervous system. The wonderful and mysterious power of consciousness works behind the success of positive visualization. The secret is this. Whatever you hold in your imagination and believe to be true, gains materiality. It means if you visualize or imagine something in your mind's eye and really believe in its existence, it will come to existence. Visualization works better when you are relaxed.

There are many techniques to integrate yoga and positive visualization. One such simple and effective method is to visualize the whole body as light energy. Visualize specific parts or glands of the body as made of, or filled with a soothing stream of light. It will help to increase the blood circulation and heal the body by sending an extra supply of vital energy to that part of the body.

Using Breathing as the Bridge

Breath is the bridge that connects our body and mind; it makes the body and mind one, illumining both, and bringing peace and calm. Breathing is the direct link between the body and the conscious mind and between the conscious and the subconscious mind. There are some very powerful endocrine responses to breathing. They were known, throughout the ages, to have a calming effect on the body and the mind.

For thousands of years, breathing awareness has been an integral part of the inner journey. Breathing can direct your awareness deep inside the temple of your body to awaken the inner dimension of spaciousness and silence. The energy of breathing, when experienced in the light of awareness, can help to harmonize your being at every level. Allowing your breath to take you deeper inside your being, however, requires much practice.

Each breath connects us with the environment, with the cosmos. Breathing brings us in close contact to the miraculous energies of life in and around us. Awareness of breathing can also teach us how to be present to the silence and spaciousness inside, from where the breaths originate. By learning to notice the inside and outgoing movements of your breaths, you learn to get in touch with a deeper and more conscious dimension of your being.

You can try a simple exercise right away. Sit with a straight back and gently close your eyes. Focus your awareness on the sensations of your breath. Is your breathing rough and shallow, or is it smooth and spacious? As you inhale, simply be aware that you are inhaling. As you exhale, be aware that you are exhaling. Just be aware, without any attempt to manipulate your breathing. Do it for a while. You may number your natural breathing, if you find it easier to hold your attention on breath that way. How did you feel? In the beginning, even if you find your attention drifting away to other things, do not fight. Gently bring your attention back to your breathing, when you become aware that you have been preoccupied with thoughts.

Breath is the carrier of vital energy. It is life energy, flowing in and out, invigorating every cell of your body and throwing the toxic things outside. By consciously following your breathing through the sensation it produces, you begin to open up to the power of breath. When you are ready to stop, give yourself a couple of minutes to sense the energy and peace being absorbed in all the cells of your body; pay particular attention to your spine from the bottom to the top.

Then bring your awareness back to the whole sensation of your just sitting and breathing.

Try this exercise for fifteen minutes or so, at least three times a day. It will help you to be free from the cobwebs of automatic thoughts and emotional reactions. It will enable you to live with clarity in the present moment. Over the time, this simple exercise may bring you in contact with the peaceful and non-judgemental silence within your inner being, the consciousness of which will make you free from all external turmoil. This is one of the safest and most powerful breathing exercises. It has its root in the teachings of Buddhism and other ancient spiritual traditions.

Witnessing: Way to Inner Freedom

Witnessing is the way of the seers, the way of all the Buddhas. When you are able to watch yourself, you will be able to know yourself. When you know yourself, you will go beyond the land of sorrow. This was the message of the Upanishads. This was the message of the Buddha. This was the message of Lao Tzu. The saying, "Know thyself," was also written on the temple of the oracle at Delphi in ancient Greece. You need to understand yourself on all levels. However, it is easier said than done. How do you actually do it? You need to study your own self on three levels of action, speech, and mind. In this path, you have to be aware, open and receptive to new insights; you have to search with the objectivity and clarity of a scientist. If you can proceed in this way, the mysteries of the inner world will be open to you.

This practice of self-study is known as *swadhyaya,* in the Sanskrit. It has been glorified in the Bhagvad Gita and Yoga sutras of Patanjali, as the way to Self-realization. *Swa* in Sanskrit means self and *Adhyaya* means study. How do you study yourself? You study yourself through aware observation on all levels of your body, thoughts, habits, emotions, sensations, intellect, and the deeper sense of being. It is said that, by observing others you become wise, and by observing yourself you become enlightened.

This art of witnessing yourself is an ancient practice pursued through countless centuries by the seekers of truth. The first real step to the inner journey is learning to witness yourself in a detached spirit. To awaken the guru within, you need to detach yourself from the body, mind and intellect. By exploring and understanding your thoughts, emotions and habit patterns, you will know that they are not your real self. You will grow the ability to detach yourself from them. Your ability to interact and communicate with others will improve, as a result. Only when you have carefully studied your own internal states, the knowledge of your inner light begins to dawn.

No one and nothing outside of you can give you salvation, or free you from the misery. You have to light your own lamp. You have to enlighten yourself. You have to know the miniature universe that you yourself are. Sitting silently, quietly, you learn to witness yourself, your own body, feelings, and emotions.

In this practice, you need to behave with your mind as its best friend. Do not be judgemental. Do not be rude or critical. Do not try to control. Just observe with a detached and innocent spirit of a scientist, with rational objectivity.

As you learn to observe your body, mind and feelings, your understanding of the mechanical nature of their working grows. Slowly you will be able to discover the automatic patterns of your behavior. The reasons behind your fears or worries and many other secrets of the body and mind, hitherto unknown, will be revealed to you. The reason, why you act or react in a certain way in a certain situation, will be clear to you. If you continue with this self-observation, you will be surprised to notice, probably for the first time in your life, that almost in every situation, you have a choice as to how you may think, speak `or act. Every situation in life presents us with an array of choices. An alert person is aware of those choices. An unaware person is not.

When you learn to observe yourself, previously what used to be an automatic reaction, seemingly so obvious now seems like a mere choice which you are free to opt for or not. As you become more and more alert and aware, you become conscious of your choices. This is so much liberating. You are no longer dictated by the automatic mechanical impulses of the body and mind.

Suppose, someone says something unbecoming to you. It creates a painful sensation within you. That is very natural. Previously your automatic reaction to it would be striking back with some sharp comment. Now, that you are more alert, you are not in a hurry to strike back. You clearly see that, you have choices regarding your response to it. As you grow a certain distance from your thoughts and emotions, your reaction do not come out automatically, without your control. Now you find much time at your disposal to weigh the choices of your possible reaction. You have time to ponder on the possible outcome of your response, or to see the motivation of the person behind saying so. Perhaps, you recognize his suffering, helplessness or worry that made him behave in that way. In any case, you are free to choose appropriate words that would convey your disappointment without aggravating the suffering of both of you.

There is a well-known anecdote related to the life of the Buddha. Once, the Buddha was out for begging. While he was passing through a certain village, a Brahmin, who was enraged upon him, approached him and began to slander him. Buddha sat their calmly, quietly waiting for the Brahmin to finish it all. After some time, the Brahmin came to his sense. He was stunned by the quiet forbearance of the Buddha. In his sheer astonishment, he forgot about his anger. He asked the Buddha, how he could manage to maintain such a calm demeanour upon being insulted so much. The Buddha replied with a counter question. He asked, what the Brahmin was supposed to do if he visited a friend with some gift that the friend refused to accept. Obviously then, there would be nothing to do other than taking the gift back with him, was the answer of the Brahmin. The Buddha said with a smile that he had learnt to make the choice of not accepting certain gifts such as those brought by the Brahmin.

If somebody wants to give you something undesirable, you have freedom of choice for not accepting that. If somebody says that, you are bad, you have the freedom of not accepting such a negative suggestion. You have the freedom to respond in a measured way without losing your clarity and composure.

Our self-study may take us to the deeper territory of our mind. We come to realize that, the mind gives reality to any experience we might have. Through self-study, the mind becomes mature, quiet and peaceful, that makes it fit for meditation or moving deeper inside. Witnessing makes you a master. Who is a master? A master is a person who is free from the slavery of the blind impulses of body and mind. Witnessing makes you stay aligned with your inner Guru, the eternal master of all beings.

Observe Three States of Consciousness

As you witness the states of your consciousness, you will find that everyday your consciousness passes through three states, viz., the waking state, the dream state and the state of deep sleep. We have the waking consciousness, the dream consciousness, and the deep-sleep consciousness. If you study these three phases of your existence, the secret of your existence will be revealed to you.

You will find that the so-called reality and solidity of your body in the waking state can be in doubt. Mind can manufacture any numbers of bodies in the dream, which exhibit the same solidity and reality, so long as the dream lasts. In your dream, your waking body is totally absent for you and you impose your identity on a dream body, which you take to be yourself during that period. Though the dream body was a 'dream body', manufactured by the mind, you did not question the reality of the dream body, so long as the dream was there. In your dream, you enjoy and suffer the fate of the dream body that is as unreal as the dream is.

Again, during the dreamless phase of sleep, you do not feel any body whatsoever, notwithstanding the fact that your physical body was lying there all the same. The deep-sleep consciousness expresses itself as a peaceful nothingness, experienced as not knowing anything. A persistent study of these states raises many questions within you and many insights come as a result.

Through witnessing these states, you come to know that you are more than your body, senses, thoughts and emotions. You may realize that, consciousness is the essence of your being. Then you may begin to see that, everything you experience is happening within your consciousness. All the experiences, thoughts and emotions float in consciousness as clouds float in the sky.

Locate the Source of a Thought

If you have a strong desire or an obstinate thought, identify it. Do not label it as good or bad. Sit quietly for a moment, and then try to locate the source of that thought within the body. Do not try to figure it out. Do not try to name it. Just put your whole attention on the source of that thought or the desire in your body. Every thought produces a certain sensation in the body. Each thought and emotion has a physical counterpart to it. If you succeed to hold your attention at the source wherefrom the thought arises, for a sufficiently long time, a miracle will happen. Abandoning the thought, as you put your attention on the source, entire energy of your thought or emotion will be transformed into nothingness, and peace will follow with the thought melted away.

Abide as Non-Doer

The inner Guru is the eternal witness of all the actions performed by the body and all the thoughts generated by the mind. It is the non-doer, whose silent nod of approval moves the whole creation. When you learn to detach yourself from your body and mind, you can abide as non-doer of actions. This practice aligns you with the inner Guru.

When your body is doing things like changing the postures, eating, standing, or walking, know that the Nature is doing everything. Body and mind are instruments of Nature; they are parts of the Nature, as we have discussed earlier. As a part of the Nature, it is interacting with a constantly changing Nature as the cosmic whole. Be a witness of your body doing everything as a part of the Nature. Actions flow effortlessly as the natural tendency of the body and the mind, while you abide as a non-doer, expecting nothing, hoping nothing, regretting nothing. Doing everything, abide as a non-doer.

Thus, gradually, the notion of you as a body begins to leave, even if for a short while in the beginning. Then you can easily see that the cosmic whole is the sole doer. This understanding, when naturally dawns on you in course of your inner journey, it can change your life.

If you can abide as a non-doer of actions, it will throw open all the doors of the mind. Witnessing will come. Surrender will happen spontaneously. Flow of grace will pervade your inner being with the light that floods the sky before the sunrise.

Ancient and Advanced Practices

There are many ancient practices, which, in ancient times, were taught only to the advanced practitioners of meditation by competent teachers of the path. Nowadays, knowledge is available to everybody with little or almost no effort. There are books available on every topic, and meditation courses are taught even on the internet. Nevertheless, the information supplied by the books can be converted to wisdom only by ardent and consistent practice, and written materials can seldom substitute the experience and proficiency of a competent teacher. Now we are going to discuss some of the most ancient practices that, if practiced correctly, could be pivotal in awakening the inner Guru, the fountainhead of joy, clarity and peace. Before starting these practices, make sure that you are in good health and have a mind without agitation.

Practice to Awaken the Sushumna

This core practice has its roots in ancient yoga and Tantra scriptures. It was secretly taught by ancient teachers of the path of inner light.

The word 'Sushumna' describes a state of undisturbed joy and calmness. When the energy moves through the 'Sushumna', the central energy-channel, which is also named as 'Saraswati', the river of nectar begins to flow. Then, the mind attains to a state of spontaneous joy, peace and calmness. Such a still mind is necessary to travel in to the deeper realm of consciousness.

To begin the practice of awakening the 'Susumna', Sit quietly cross-legged, either on the floor or on a chair. Be sure that your spine is erect yet supple. Keep your hands folded gently together on your lap or keep your palms down on your knees. As you sit, sense your weight being supported by the earth and feel the whole sensation of your body sitting and breathing.

Now bring your awareness at the centre of your crown, the place called the 'Brahma Randhra'. Stay there for a while, and notice if you feel any sensations there. Bring the awareness down through the frontal part of your body, until you reach your throat. Breathe a few times through the throat producing a soft friction in the larynx. Be aware of the friction in the throat and the energy moving in that area.

Now continue to move your awareness down to the chest, to your belly, and further down, until you reach the toe and soles of your feet. Feel every sensation on the way, neither embracing any sensation nor ignoring them. Now begin the journey of awareness again from the sole of your feet up through the back portion of your body until you reach your crown. Do it a few times, in a relaxed manner.

Next, bring your awareness on the spinal column. Slowly, go up and down the spine a few times centring your awareness on the main chakras or subtle nerve centres along the spine. Now feel the spine from the coccyx up to the point at the back of your forehead and see if you can sense the energy within it. After you bring your awareness on the spine and feel the subtle flow of energy within it, you are ready to enter the inner shrine of the temple that the body is.

Now, bring your awareness on the breath as it is felt within the nostrils, as we discussed in the previous exercise. Feel the incoming and outgoing breaths in the middle between the nostrils. As you continue to breathe, become aware of the places in your body where you feel subtle tensions. These are the places where the energy flow has become stuck in the body. Allow yourself to breathe right through these places.

After some time, focus your awareness on the bridge between the two nostrils. As you continue to do this process for a while, you will notice that both the nostrils are flowing freely. It is the indication that the Sushumna has began to awaken. When both the nostrils are flowing freely, it is called the Sandhya, the juncture point at the middle between the day and the night.

Once you are established in this experience, with consistent practice, the mind becomes one pointed, focussed, inward and tranquil. Breath becomes thinner and thinner, and ultimately you transcend the mind. As the 'Sushumna' awakens, your connection with your inner Guru will be established. An undercurrent of inner joy will be felt as a result. With this inner joy, the mind learns to be happy within itself. All the external distractions are removed, and meditation flows by itself. Awakening the 'Sushumna' is the most important practice to awaken the inner Guru.

Working with the Third Eye

After the 'Sushumna' is awakened, soon you will feel subtle sensations at the point of the third eye, just above the point between the eyebrows. Then, you will be in a position to work with the third eye. Before that, it is dangerous to work with the third eye. Never try to do it unless you are sure that 'Sushumna' has awakened, giving you complete mastery over your mind. Without awakening the 'Sushumna' and having purity of thought, working with the third eye could bring physical and mental diseases such as headache, migraine, restlessness, nervousness and even insanity.

The third eye is the door to pure consciousness. It is the seat of the supreme Self, manifesting as your inner Guru. Developing the third eye is a direct way to expand your consciousness and fathom the mystery of the existence. You look at the centre of your inner world when you look through your third eye. Turning your eyes inward, looking from this point, affects your pituitary gland, and allows the energy to flow strongly. When you learn to look through your third eye, the impressions coming from the external world will be received through your third eye before they reach your mind. They will be filtered and purified by the third eye.

There are many methods to focus the awareness on the third eye. The third eye meditations works on the sixth centre of consciousness, known as the 'Ajna' Chakra. When you focus your awareness on the third eye, a meditative state follows almost spontaneously and instantly.

The following method is simple but powerful. Sit with your spine upright but relaxed. Gently close your eyes and exhale deeply for a few times in a relaxed manner. Now focus your awareness on the middle of your forehead around the area just above the middle of your eyebrows. This is position that is mystically known as the third eye. Lift your eyes slightly upward, as if, to gaze at that point. Look upwards towards your third eye, keeping the eyes closed. It is, as if, you are trying to look at the back of your third eye, with eyes closed. You do not need to raise your eyes too high. If you notice your eyes fluttering, then simply relax your gaze and allow your eyes to find their natural and most balanced position to gaze at the point between the eyebrows. It should be relatively effortless, though you may need to put a little effort in the beginning.

If you notice after awhile that your focus has waned, just be sure to softly bring your eyes back to gaze at the point between the eyebrows and keep your eyes closed, or half-closed. Allow them to rest there comfortably, without strain. At a particular position of your eyeballs, both of your eyes will become motionless, as if, a force from above was working to keep them still. That is the point for the eyes to abide.

This is a special meditative posture that has helped many people move deeper into meditation. By placing your attention there, you are sending the energy of your focused attention to the Pituitary and Pineal glands, which in turn release Neuropeptides, the chemicals, which invoke a relaxation response and allow you to move deeper into meditation. These Pituitary and Pineal glands are master glands, which also release hormones that are conducive to health and healing.

After you have been able to keep your attention here for a while, try to locate any sensation there. Do not imagine anything. Just be relaxed and aware of any sensation at the area of your third eye, as you breathe normally. As you do so, start counting down from hundred to one, in your mind, slowly, at a relaxed pace, keeping your awareness centerd at the third eye. By the time you reach the number one in the backward counting, be aware again if you can feel any sensation around your third eye. Maintain awareness of this point. After some time as you reach a state of stillness of eyes, you will feel, as if, you can see your thoughts appearing before you as a screen.

Now begin to notice the thoughts and feelings, as they arise. Simply witness them without judgment. Third eye is the place of witnessing. It is the royal seat of the witness within you. While the external eyes are meant to see the ordinary things of the world, the third eye is meant for inner or psychic vision and witnessing. Hence, third eye is the gate for our journey from mundane human existence to our real being as the being of light.

As you witness your thoughts and emotions, notice that you are not the feelings or the thoughts, as they appear and disappear on your mental screen. You are the spacious screen of awareness, which hold them. You are the conscious witness that is silently watching them.

The more you are able to pull back into this silent witness, the more the subtle and powerful space of your consciousness opens up within you, which ultimately dissolve the old thought patterns and habits. When the meditation is finished, allow yourself to sit quietly for a few minutes, which will allow you to readily release whatever conscious or subconscious material came up during the meditation.

As you do this exercise regularly, at a certain point, all the thoughts will stop. You will be able to experience the vast thoughtless realm of your consciousness, which will make you free. You will come to know yourself as the witnessing silence that you are. This golden silence of witnessing, this vast thoughtless realm of consciousness is the glimpse of the infinite within you. It is the reality of who you are, beyond thoughts and forms, beyond space and time. This is your immortal being, made of pure silence, which the weapons can not destroy, fire can not burn, water can not wet, air can not dry. This is your real being which even the death can never take away from you.

When you reach this state of pure silence, you will want to be at this state for a while. This is an extremely peaceful state to abide. Remain there as long as you like. Then slowly shift your eyes to their normal positions. Come back to the normal state of consciousness by being aware of your breathing, your body and surroundings. Inhale and exhale deeply for a few times. Now slowly open your eyes. This third eye meditation is a very powerful practice in awareness.

However, any meditation that directly works on the third eye is better to do under the guidance of an experienced teacher. When the 'Sushumna' is awakened, the third eye centre begins to open. With a little practice, soon the mind and intellect is absorbed in the divine light of the inner Guru, and the state of Samadhi is experienced.

Find the Inner Source of Joy

This is another key practice that helps in awakening the guru within. Whenever you are filled with joy, whenever you are satisfied for something, try to find the inner source of that joy or satisfaction. Your inner Guru is the source of all bliss, sacred or profane, as the mind may interpret it. Suppose you are satisfied and happy after taking your breakfast. Sit silently for a moment and then turn your attention inward. With a relaxed mind, try to locate the source of the satisfaction. Fix your mind there with full awareness and then feel as if your whole body and mind is flooded with that satisfaction. Do not think yourself as an individual being. Merge yourself with that blissful essence of your being. You may do this experiment with any blissful experience in life.

Meditate on the Luminous Inner Sun

As we have known, the inner Guru exists within as pure witnessing. It is the golden light of being that knows everything inside and outside of our body. Its golden orb contains the whole universe within it.

To meditate on this inner Sun, sit quietly with the eyes gently closed. Feel your breath entering the nostril and going down to your heart, and then, coming up to go out of the nostrils. Be aware of this process for some time. Try to feel the breath, the warmth of it, as it flows. Now, visualize the rising Sun in front of your nostrils. Feel that it is entering within with the incoming breath and going down to your heart. The Sun settles there. With the outgoing breath, all the darkness of your being comes out, driven by the rays of the Sun. Continue to see and feel the Sun within you. After some time, feel that the golden orb of the Sun is spreading until it covers all your limbs. Feel that the orb envelops your body and continues to expand until it holds the whole universe within it. The Sun within your heart is at the centre of this universe. You are the centre of the universe. Extend your love, prayer and good will to all the beings of the entire universe. This meditation has unlimited potential to expand your consciousness and awaken the guru within you.

Attune with Inner Silence

This is a core practice and can be the only practice, when you are ready for it. Practice of silence is a direct way to awaken the guru within you. The only way to attune to the silence of your being is to stop doing everything else. Everything means everything. Just be silent. If you can do that, it is the most amazing thing you can ever discover.

To attune to the silence, you must start with the experience of the coarser sounds. Whenever you find some time, make yourself calm and receptive to the sounds that are going on in your environment. Listen to the sounds around you reaching out as far as you can. Try not to miss any sound that is going on. Do not make any judgement as to what, or which type of sound is coming to you. Make yourself available and open to all the sounds in your surroundings, as and when they happen. Go on listening, without labelling them mentally. Focus on the sound in its purity. Do not focus on the words, if any sound of a conversation happens to come to your ears.

Listen to every sound. Be aware of the silent spaces between the sounds. Listen to the silence. Listen to the sound of the silence. That is the voice of your inner Guru. As you continue to do this, your breathing will become slow and subtle.

Slowly, you will grow a knack of it and you will notice that, by this method a gap is being created between the incessant streams of thoughts in your mind. That is the beginning of listening to the inner silence. Open your heart to that silence. If you go on pursuing with this method, one day, when you are absolutely silent, receptive and open, the grace, splendour and luminosity of the inner Guru will flood you with a sense of all pervading fullness of being as the bliss filled inner music of silence. Then, you will know that this silence is the truest thing about who you are.

Renounce False Identities

Enlightenment happens when you are ready to let go of the false identities spun around you. We have many layers in our personalities. The word personality comes from the Greek word 'Persona' that literally means masks. Masks mean false identities. Our family, society, and profession create one after another mask on our original being. In the Zen tradition of Buddhism, enlightenment is known as knowing your real face. If you really want to realize your inner Guru or your real Self, be prepared to abandon all your false identities.

This was the true purpose of renunciation. This was the reason why monks and recluses renounced their friends, family and society to live in their forest dwellings or hermitages. What they really intended to do is renounce their past and future. That external renunciation was just symbolic of an intention to abandon their false social identities. It was just the preparation of moving beyond the mind, keeping aside all the masks, abandoning all thoughts of the past and future. In fact, external renunciation is not an absolute necessity for moving beyond, if you are ready to be a no-body in the midst of your daily life.

Being nobody means abandoning all the false identities and abiding in your real nature. Then, whatever might be your external status, whatever might be your action or occupation, they never touch you, just as the water can not wet the Lotus-leaf.

The mind, you know, is always afraid to become nobody, because it is born of the idea, 'I am the body'. Hence, being no-body threatens its own existence. It does not like that. However, renunciation, in essence, is all about being nobody, in the essential sense of the term. Renunciation really means totally renouncing the past, to be born anew every moment.

Renunciation, after all, happens in your inner world. It happens inside of you, when it really happens. It does not happen out of apathy, fear, disgust, or indifference to the world. It would be absolutely irrational and meaningless if it would have to happen through those negative emotions. In reality, it happens spontaneously as you move towards the higher realm of your being; it happens as you become more alert and aware, ready to move beyond the mind. It is just, as if, you are leaving the lower stairs and the ground floor in order to go upstairs to the first floor. You do not need to make much fuss about that because this higher realm of consciousness is your own inner being that already exists within you.

Renunciation prepares the ground. Then awakening happens and the flower of thousand petals blossom in the ray of the inner Sun. It happens when you are ready. It happens when you are ready to be silent and alone, abiding within your own being. Ask yourself if you are ready for that, if you are ready to take the plunge in to the unknown. Are you prepared to let go of any significance or meaning you have projected onto persons, events or situations in your life? Could you imagine being entirely complete and utterly at peace, with no need for anything or anybody? Could you just allow the feeling of being utterly and perfectly complete arise effortlessly in your awareness? If you could do that, you are ready to take the ultimate plunge in to the unknown.

If you are ready for that, then, set aside a time exclusively to be alone with yourself. As you learn to attune with the inner silence of your being, mentally abandon everything that exists in your life at the periphery of your being. Everything means everything, your possessions, roles, responsibility, social status and all relations. Discard all the opinions people cherish about you, all the roles you are playing in social, professional and family life. They are all peripheral, and do not have to do anything with what you are at the core of your being. Remain in this detached, aloof and solitary state of mind for the assigned time of meditation.

Rest within yourself, feeling whatever sensations are coming on your way, such as the feeling of the breeze, of the sounds coming from a distance or the sensation of your own breath. Do not make any judgement about anything. When you are silent, peaceful and choicelessly aware of everything in and around you, you will find that the nature of this awareness is very innocent, almost childlike. Stay with this feeling of childlike being as long as you like. Thus, you begin to reclaim the paradise of your childhood for some moments. "Unless you are like a child, you can not enter the heaven of God"!

Over time, as you continue to do this, resting and relaxing within yourself, with a silent, receptive and open heart, you will gradually find that the experience of this awareness is very spacious, almost like the sky. As if, everything in the moment was unfolding in the sky of your own awareness. This feeling is very liberating. As your mind gets more and more still, you let everything be in your awareness, without making a comment or judgement about what happens.

Then, one day, sitting silently with closed eyes, your whole being will suddenly be flooded with a profound feeling of unity that contains the whole universe within it. Everything you see is brimming with this consciousness. You realize that, you and this consciousness are not different.

Let this realization sink deep within you. Let it flow within you through all you think, speak and do. Then you will be ever connected to this infinite source of auspiciousness, and the day will come when the thin mental line of demarcation between you and your inner Guru as the infinite sky of consciousness, will gradually blur to fade away forever, making you feel at one with the source of fulfilment.

Spiritual Awakening is not something, which transforms us into a being that we are not, but rather it awakens us to the truth of who we really are. Our real nature is pure consciousness and our inner Guru is the all-pervading consciousness that shines in everything.

Become Aware of your Awareness

Can you make yourself aware of your awareness? In the practice of witnessing, you learn to witness your body, your sensations, thoughts, feelings and emotions. The next step in witnessing is to become aware of the thoughtless, bare space of awareness, which witnesses the thoughts arising within it. Just shift your awareness to become aware of the sense of presence that is aware within you. See what is it that is aware of being aware. Do not try to get any answer. Answers are all supplied by the mind, which is a false entity itself. Even if, the answer comes as “I am becoming aware”, try to see who this “I” is, that is becoming aware. (The body, as an inert object, made of flesh, blood and bones can not become aware.) So, abandon all mental activities, by refusing to accept any explanation supplied by the mind. Just see and silently feel it.

Offer a Selfless Prayer or a Blessing

End all your practices everyday with a silent selfless prayer or blessing. This is a very profound practice. At the end of your meditation, when you normally abide in a peaceful state, it is very powerful to offer a silent, heart-felt blessing to your loved ones, friends, teachers, and to all people of the world in general. This is very much beneficial for you, because, as you do so, the deeper layers of your being are imprinted with compassion and love that are stepping stones to reach the higher levels of consciousness. Moreover, in this world of cause and effect, you can not give anything without receiving anything. Therefore, you receive, as you give good will and compassion. The more you practice this, both in meditation and during the day, the more your meditation deepens.

Practices for Daily Living

In the preceding section, we have discussed a set of practices that, if patiently pursued, over time, would ultimately help you to merge with your inner Guru as the very essence of your being. Do not practice them haphazardly. Do not hasten to the next practice, immediately after you have started one. When you feel that you are ready to move to the next practice, begin to include them in your lifestyle. The rule remains the same. See for yourself, what brings you joy, relaxation and clarity. That would be the right set of practices for you.

Now we are going to discuss some essential practices to be followed in your daily life. These practices are essential to tread the path of light. They are necessary if you want to develop inner clarity and freedom. When you practice them in a conscious manner, with understanding and patience developed over time through sincere and sustained effort, they will throw open the door of the highest realm of consciousness for you. Then meditation follows with effortless ease.

Be Courageous

Strength is the essence of life. Strength is the beginning of spirituality. It is in difficult times in life that your mettle in known. When everything is going on smoothly, even a fool can behave like the wise, a weakling can manage to maintain a bold and smiling demeanour. It is when things go wrong, your strength and wisdom is on test. It is on such times that your strength is known by your capacity to remain unperturbed, to speak and act wisely, with patience and clarity of mind, to respond to the situation consciously in an unhurried but determined manner. This is called the strength of character that separates you from the ordinary crowd who reacts and behaves in an almost unconscious manner when faced by a disagreeable situation.

You are strong and courageous, when you align yourself with your inner Guru. Courage and inner strength comes when you trust in the infinite intelligence residing within you as your inner Guru. Trusting your inner Guru helps you to believe in yourself, but not simply in a part of yourself as the body and mind that appear on the surface of your being as the tip of the iceberg. It is trusting on yourself in your totality. It is a trust on your greater, interior self that is limitless in power and possibility.

Never forget that the human body of yours is the shrine of the highest and the most divine. Make it a practice to be aware of a higher presence within you that is kind, calm, self-assured, balanced and peaceful. It exists within you as the still silent witness of everything you do, speak and think. It also witnesses the drama of life as it unfolds with calm poise and fearlessness. It is the image of God within you. The whole universe belongs to this power of guru within. Never let this body mind do, speak or think anything that does not fit this noblest and most dignified presence within you.

Learning to be conscious of this presence within you makes you courageous. You may quietly affirm in your mind, "I am, in essence, one with the infinite consciousness as my inner Guru who protects and guides my body, mind and intellect to lead me towards happiness, harmony and fulfilment", if you find it helpful to remind you of the Presence within you.

Unconditional trust on your inner Guru makes you so strong, that nothing, nobody, no situation, however daunting, can take away your inner peace, poise and resolve to succeed. This gives you courage because you are being true to that which is the most noble, most powerful and most precious within you and every being on earth. Then your faith brings the whole world on your side because your inner Guru is the Self of all. Then, you become almost invincible under every situation that life may present.

Courage itself is enough to connect and align you with the infinite potential of your inner Guru, even if, you do not consciously remember to do so. Courage is the secret through which the energy in your navel centre opens to connect you with the cosmic energy. Courage makes you an achiever in every field of action. Courage makes you see the sunny side in every situation. It makes you think only for the best, work only for the best and expect only the best in all circumstances.

Inscrutable and mysterious are the ways of life, but, those who persist in all circumstances, however daunting they may seem, win in the end. Nature gives way to the strong and the courageous. Know this, and never give up. Do not get disappointed when things seem disappointing. Keep your eyes single upon the purpose. Make a resolve to yourself to remain as strong, determined and positive during the trials of life, as you are in the sunniest hours of your life. When your resolve is strong by trust on your inner Guru, nature will surely bow down before that resolve. The things and forces that were initially against you will take delight in serving you.

Remember that challenges in our lives make us grow in strength. Challenges make us evolve faster only if we remember that every cloud has a silver lining behind it, and every crisis carries within its bosom an opportunity. Whenever you feel that situations, things or people are overwhelming you, invoke your inner Presence, resolve to remain strong and courageous by this invincible power within you and victory will be yours.

Love and Care, Give and Share

We are one in the infinite consciousness. All the waves are part of the same ocean. They are one with the ocean. On each level of our existence, we are connected with, and dependent on, others. Even as the body and mind, our existence is dependent on other beings in the plant and animal kingdom. For example, the Sun is the source of our energy by which the physiological activities of our bodies run; but, the whole of the animal kingdom, including us, the human beings, are incapable of directly assimilating sunlight in our body. Only the plants are endowed with the capacity to store the energy of the Sun within their body through the process of photosynthesis. They are at the lowest end of the food chain from which the whole of the animal kingdom derives nutrition and the solar energy necessary to generate energy for their survival.

Likewise, we are connected to the earth through food and water. We, all of us, rich and poor, saint and sinner alike, breathe in the same recycled air in the atmosphere. We are but tiny parts of an indivisible whole. Hence, by loving and helping others, we can not but love and help ourselves. By sharing what we have with others, we are actually giving it back to ourselves. This law is ancient and infallible. So, not as a doctrine, dogma or maxim, but for our own good, we should embrace this ancient law of life.

This law is the law of loving, caring, giving and sharing with all the fellow beings on the planet. Love is the divine light that can melt away all inner blockages. Love heals our being at all levels. Modern medical science and psychology has also proved that love is a great healing force. Love and other such emotions that cause expansion of consciousness act as antidotes to the blockages created by hatred, anger, fear, anxiety, stinginess and other negative emotions. The negative emotions create resistances and generate toxic chemicals, which are transformed, over the time, to subtle blockages in the neuromuscular systems that manifests as various physical and neurological diseases as the end result.

Love is the panacea for almost all diseases. Love heals the body, mind and nervous system. When you bear an attitude of love, caring and sharing, you feel relaxed and peaceful, and the inner light shines bright. Only a loving heart can know happiness. Being loving and caring makes you perfectly aligned and in tune with your inner Guru. Being loving and caring to our fellow beings, we pay our deepest respect to our inner Guru, the true guru of all.

Live in the Moment

A royal way to come out of the chatter of the mind is to focus the consciousness on what is happening now. Only living in this moment has the power to unlock the hidden power of consciousness that is the potential of success and fulfilment both in material and spiritual sense. Living in this moment does not mean that you do not plan, or, you do not learn from your past mistakes. That is a foolish interpretation of this most delicate and subtle principle of life. Let your mind plan for the future; let your mind train itself from the experiences it meets. However, we should not be trapped in the obsessive and unconstructive thoughts of the past and the future.

As we learn to be conscious of each moment, appreciating each moment, the unnecessary chatter of the mind stops, to reveal the clarity of our inner being. Past and future both are parts of the imaginations of the mind. This moment is like a precious pearl on the garland of eternity. Living in the moment has enormous potential to change your life.

This moment is the fullest and purest expression of consciousness that you are experiencing. Everything we experience is unfolding in this moment. Anything you say, do, feel or experience this moment is an expression of consciousness. When you start to live in the moment, which is untainted by the thoughts of the past, you live as the consciousness, naturally. Living as the consciousness, you are living at the source; living as the source.

See how you feel when you only focus on what is happening right now. As you continually do this, you will see yourself starting to enjoy the process. When you do this, you are automatically stepping out of the mind. Thoughts will be fewer and fewer, until there is none.

Bliss can really happen only in such a state of no-mind. When you learn to live in the present moment, gradually you learn to relax and rest in the silence of your being, instead of remaining caught up in thoughts. Inner Guru reveals itself as the golden silence of your being of unlimited bliss, only when you are absolutely at the present and not moving to anywhere else other than the present.

Remember Impermanence

When we live in the moment, we are prepared to welcome the changes that come in our lives. Accepting the changes is not enough. We need to welcome and embrace changes. When you remember the sacred truth of impermanence of everything, you can welcome changes. Change means the end of something and beginning of another. Some changes in our lives are welcomed by the mind, while some are not. When we remember impermanence, we live at ease with life, gliding effortlessly through it, through the peak of joys and the valley of sorrows.

Through impermanence, the Nature is constantly worshipping the inner Guru, the changeless and eternal background on which life and death are happening, as images appear on a screen. Between every change, between every end and every beginning, there is a gap. This gap reveals the inner guru as pure consciousness that is devoid of any objectification. Hence, impermanence is the sacred law of nature, the law that reveals the gaps between two consecutive events, things, situations or thoughts. Through this sacred law, life is worshipping the inner Guru, the only constant presence behind this impermanence.

Landmarks on the Path

This human life is so very precious. In this very life is hidden the potential for manifesting our godly being, the highest evolution of our consciousness. Once you undertake this path, make yourself committed to manifesting your highest potential. No commitment to any doctrine, dogma, faith or ideology is more precious than your commitment to yourself, to your highest spiritual being.

If you are really growing by following a certain path, you will find yourself growing in peace, stability, calmness and purity, emitting positive energies of love, kindness, forgiveness and compassion for all. Level of happiness is another indicator of your progress on the path. If your happiness and joy is increasing, you will be sure that you are progressing. You will feel that you are full with love and compassion. Your mind will be celebrating each moment. A higher order and deeper sense of wellbeing will naturally emerge in your life.

While you will be more caring and compassionate towards people in general, you will be able to act with a certain detachment and your dependence on any external situations, things or people will largely decrease. Ultimately, the inner Guru will be awakened when the false sense of individuality is merged to be one with the ever-present cosmic Sun of bliss that resides within all the beings. This happens when through sincere and sustained effort, the mind becomes pure and the consciousness is fully liberated from identification with a limited form.

Ultimately, as you are awakened to the light within, all the darkness is removed like a bad dream that no longer exists upon waking up. All the wrong identifications are gone and you re-discover your reality as the infinite consciousness that is of the nature of pure peace.

Nevertheless, we must remember that the inner Guru existing within and without of us is sovereign in nature. It is never limited by the law of cause and effect, which rules our world in the space-time trajectory. No method or process can force the Sun to rise. No method or process can force the inner Guru to awaken in the sky of our consciousness. All the methods and practices only help us to open the door, step out of the confine of the mind, and patiently wait for the Sun to rise. As the inner Sun rises, the light will overflow melt and dissolve our being within its all-consuming Grace.

Chapter Seven

AN AWAKENED LIVING

"When you work, you are a flute through whose heart the whispering of the hours turns to music."

--- Kahlil Gibran, The Prophet

The Singing Bell of Time

Do you have the courage to open your heart,
Open to this moment, filled with fresh Life?
Wonder and amazement,
Joys and regret,
Excitement and monotony,
Memories so many.

Mystery of birth, grandeur of youth
Radiance of health and gloom of death;
Life's endless verity.
A garland of moments, precious and rare
Shimmering like stars, everything we care
Dancing on thread of eternity.

Panorama of life, the play going on

The magic screen of time.
Vanished like a dream, yesterday is gone,
Memories still aflame.

Tomorrow, another dream,
A mind-movie, going on and on
Made of bubbles and foam of hope;
Live 'today', till it is gone.

Do not be a miser, celebrate the moment
One after another, it comes in torrent;
The bell of time keeps singing.
Live now and here, smiling and breathing,
Calm and mindful, loving and caring,
Only 'today' remains for living.

Celebrating joy, celebrating sorrow,
In sweet surrender melt today and tomorrow
With a singing heart or a tearful smile,
Live with love overflowing.

Live awakened, the time has come
Flowers of minds are blossoming.
Far and near, the fragrance spreading
Petals open up, in oneness amazing;
The bell of time singing happy song
Comes an era of awakening.

~:~

Enlightenment is not something to be attained in a remote future, though normally, the ego-mind likes to keep it that way. The reality is that, truth is already present, here and now, shining in its pristine glory. It is the awareness of your very being, devoid of all unnecessary and meaningless accumulations of the past.

Mind likes to postpone it because it threatens the mind's own survival. Mind likes to paint all sorts of colorful imaginations about it, as it validates the mind's own existence and usefulness. Truth is so much self-illuminating that the mind, with all its vain chattering, need not be present to imagine it. Nevertheless, mind always likes to keep the enlightenment in a future mode. It also wants to be present at the time of enlightenment, in order to experience and explain it. But that never happens.

The paradox is that, the Ultimate reality and mind can never co-exist, because mind is a false identity, which goes on chattering to validate, explain, judge, accept or reject any experience, according to its own interpretation; whereas the Ultimate reality is revealed in pure silence, when mind, the thinking machine is completely at rest. It may happen this very moment, if you are ready.

Live as Consciousness

Do not postpone it for future. Start living consciously from today. Be conscious of all the activities your body is going through. Try to take note of every thought passing through your mind. Find the calm center within you that is never affected by any external phenomena, and live your life from that quiet center of poise and balance within you. The more you lead a life aflame with awareness, the more you become conscious of the gaps; gaps between the thoughts, the gaps between two consecutive events. The more you are conscious of the gaps, the more you are aware of your essence, which exists in these gaps as the sky of pure consciousness.

As you are awakened to your essence, living as consciousness will be effortless for you. Ultimately, you will be one with the light of all pervading bliss consciousness forever. Then, you realize that your idea of who you are, as a small self, was an illusion. It was born out of false identification with the body, thoughts and emotions.

This realization brings a profound sense of freedom. When this understanding spreads its roots in your being, not at the level of intellect, as a result of mere analytical thinking, not at the level of mind, as information, but as the realization of the reality of who you really are, it brings a profound sense of freedom and transformation.

Living as the consciousness, you live as the source. When you live as consciousness, you flow with the moment. You live as pure experiencing at this moment, focussed in the moment, effortlessly gliding from moment to moment. You plan for the future events in the present; you remember a lesson from the past in the present, when you are required to do so. Only, you do so consciously, instead of weaving a daydream. You are not trapped in the unconscious net of nostalgia or lamentation. You live rooted in the present moment experiencing the moment as it is, and not as it should be.

Pure consciousness is pure experiencing. Our true nature is this non-doing, non-thinking consciousness. It is a state unclouded by thoughts and emotions. It is a state of clarity and bliss. As you live an awakened life, you live beyond the mind. You live in the moment as the consciousness experiencing the moment.

An awakened person is happy, no matter what life offers. Living as consciousness, you are living at the source, as the source. Then, you will begin to experience bliss for no reason at all. Consciousness is bliss and when you live as consciousness, the bliss of your being fills you from within.

Finding the Missing Link with Cosmos

As you awaken to your essence as the inner Guru, you have found the way to re-establish your missing link with the whole cosmos. You have tuned your inner instruments with the rhythm of the universe. Then you are no longer a lone entity living this life just struggling for survival.

You will know that the inner light is the missing link to our real nature that is ever perfect, stainless and of the nature of pure bliss. That is the indwelling presence in all as the Self of all. That is the knower of all. That is the source of all. It is beyond all dualities of good and bad, and it bestows supreme happiness to the person who is awakened to it.

Living as this inner essence, you find your real place in this universe. You find your body-mind as a seemingly insignificant part of a wonderful cosmic whole. Each of us is a ray of the Self-Sun that is unique, yet same with the rest. Ultimately, you find that you and this inner Sun are not different. It is more close to your true nature than any other identity you have ever cherished. This realization awakens you completely from the dream of the limited individual existence.

Non Attached to Action or Inaction

When the intuitive knowing of your real Self supersedes your notion of the little self, the little self becomes just a notion, used as a utility needed for customary convenience in daily behavior, and nothing more than that. The real Self, in whom we discover that, we live, breathe, and have our bodily beings, shines in all its splendour to fill us with its light, love and fragrance.

An enlightened life is a presence on earth that is never attached to action or inaction. You live in a state of effortless surrender and 'let go'. Whatever is naturally happening through the organs of your body, mind or speech, flows as the homage to your divine Self. You go on doing your everyday job with precision and perfection; but you remain completely non-attached to it, knowing in your heart perfectly well that the result of your work, such as success or failure, praise or blame can never affect your inner being of perfect bliss. The panorama of life flows on effortlessly before you, as a dream witnessed by you. The fruits of Karma will not touch such a person, just as the water can not wet a lotus-leaf. An awakened living is living like a flute, with divine melody of your inner Guru flowing through your body and mind.

Living in Fearlessness

When you find the deathless sky of your inner being, as your unborn and undying nature, you spontaneously begin to live fearlessly. You live in a calm dignity born of the knowledge of your immortal Self. Knowing the eternal nature of your real being, you live in peace and harmony with all that exists. When all the false identifications with the impermanent objects vanish, fearlessness will be as natural as your breath.

Self Love, the Ultimate Ecstasy

Then, only then, you will be able to, really, love. This is when you are aware that you are the same shining Sun as anybody is, veiled in the mask of individual body and mind. You will see, through the veil of individuality, the eternal Sun of love, shining deep within everybody. However, this love will be very different from that what is normally known as love. This pure love is of the nature of deep friendliness and compassion that is utterly non-possessive and non-asserting. As you are awakened to the truth of your being, you will artlessly radiate a silent love that is not an emotion but a blessedness expressing itself as a gentle benevolence towards all the existence. You will be a blessing to the existence.

This love will flow as your breath, as your glance, as your very presence. Your very presence will radiate the serene understanding of the unity of all that exists. This Self-love can be quite intoxicating in nature that melts and merges the whole universe within it.

Being of Unlimited Bliss

Bliss is inherent in the Self as fragrance is inherent in a flower. As the flower of the Self-love blossoms, bliss comes spontaneously as the fragrance. Bliss emerges from within your being, when you realize that limitless expansion of consciousness is our real nature. The limitless and infinite bliss consciousness shines as the inner Guru within our being as the essence of that unconditional love that we are made of.

In reality, we are already liberated, awakened and pure, as consciousness. There is nothing to bind us; there is nothing to taint the pristine purity of our being. You are already that which you are searching. There is an endless reservoir of joy in your heart. Living as the consciousness, you will find your real being as the being made up of an ocean of unlimited bliss.

Peace that passes all Understanding

As your sense of inner bliss deepens within you, you will find that the deepened sense of joy and bliss will actually embolden you to relax more deeply into the essence of your being. Now you should be prepared to let go of the bliss as it arises. Because whatever you cling to makes you miserable. Do not even cling to any blissful feelings that spontaneously keep arising at this time, as your inner sky becomes clear and free from obstructions. The more you let go of whatever arises, even if it is such a desirable state such as bliss, the more blissful and light you will feel, until you eventually feel a profound sense of peace and equanimity that never fades away.

Thus, one day, the door opens for the realization where even the consciousness, as you know it, will not be present to give you the objective view of this world, though you remain perfectly aware within your being. Such an experience words can hardly describe. It is the ultimate peace of not knowing anything other than the deep awareness of one's own being. It is emptiness overflowing with the fullness, where ordinary concept of being merges and melts in to non-being. It is the state of supreme peace, which passes all understanding.

All this happens without you making any special effort to make it happen. In fact, contrary to the existing notion, all efforts, after a certain point, become counterproductive to realize this restful state of effortless, unborn, undying peace that already exists within you. It is, as if, Grace unfolds to reveal itself.

Still, at the beginning, we make efforts. We meditate. We make an effort to live consciously. Ultimately, we understand that, to realize our real nature, we need to learn aware resting and relaxing within our being; this is not something you do with effort. In fact, rest and relaxation always is a state of effortlessness. It is a state of effortless being. Can you allow yourself to imagine not needing to do anything at all?

Resting and relaxing within your being happens only when you relinquish the need to do anything. Resting happens when you give up the wish to make anything happen or not happen. Resting happens only when you surrender yourself to the moment. Resting happens only when you let go of the need to become something or somebody. Resting happens when you completely renounce the urge to understand or grasp something. Resting also happens as and when you surrender to your inner Guru, the light within.

It also happens as you surrender to any moment of pure love, bliss or wonder, when the surrender is so total that you yourself disappear in to it. Then the light of pure being reveals within its bosom the vast silence and amazing emptiness as the non-being core of this existence. The essential core of our real nature is that eternal state of absolute rest, which flowers in the right season, in a right kind of soil.

That is, when the flower of nirvana blossoms within our own being, its fragrance filling us as overflowing love and peace, that has absolutely no boundary. Enlightenment is all about awakening to our real nature, and abiding by that truth with effortless ease.

Living Life in the Spirit of Celebration

Then life becomes a ceaseless song of celebration that goes on until the oil is consumed in the earthen lamp of the body. Celebration is the purpose of this creation. This creation is the Self, celebrating its own being. When you live consciously, your Self-nature asserts itself in everything you do. In every act like singing, writing, walking and even breathing, the joy of the Self peeps through. Bliss pervades all. A joyful action becomes the worship of the Self by the Self.

This life is meant to be a song of celebration. This life is meant to be a grand cosmic poetry of love, peace, and harmony. In fact, the word Universe literally means a verse of unity; 'uni' means single, or one, and 'verse' means poetry or song. This whole existence is one song of unity. The grand cosmic play of the Universe was created for the purpose of sacred purposelessness. We are the means, and we are the end, in this play of divine energy of consciousness.

In the time-honoured words of the wise Hopi Elders: "Do not look outside of yourself for a leader. The time of the lone wolf is over. Gather yourselves. Banish the word 'struggle' from your attitude and your vocabulary. All that we do now must be done in a sacred manner and in celebration. We are the ones we have been waiting for."

We are the rays of the infinite Self-Sun, coming down to earth every moment in joyful celebration of our existence. Do not wait for the realization to happen in some distant future. Do not wait for some supernatural experience to transform your life. Live as the energy of consciousness, from this very moment. You are inseparably connected with all that exists. You are inseparably connected with the all-pervading pure consciousness, your inner Guru. You are free to live this understanding this very moment. Nothing can restrict you to live the truth of who you really are.

When you live in this unity consciousness, your life becomes blessed. Your very presence becomes a blessing to the existence. Then, without doing anything, you accomplish everything. You attain to the zenith of experience in this human plane of existence. Your mundane life becomes sacred as it merges and melts with the Divine whole in the eternal song of celebration.

ABOUT THE AUTHORS

Banani Ray is a mystic, spiritual guide and author of several books on meditation, mysticism and infinite human potential. She studied and mastered the Bhagvad Gita, when she was in school, and the book became her constant companion. She adored and took Bhagvad Gita as her guide. While she was teaching in a women's college, she experienced an awakening, and underwent a massive inner transformation, which led her to undertake deep spiritual practices in the quest for realization of the ultimate truth. For the next nine years, she continued to meditate.

Ultimately, her quest motivated her to undertake austere spiritual practices and self-enquiry in solitude. For several years, she lived in Himalaya with her husband Amit, living a life dedicated to meditation and spiritual practice. Over the years, a series of mystic experiences opened up for her the door for profound realization of the underlying connectedness and oneness of all beings. She began to live her realization, sharing her wisdom and teachings with people coming to her from far and near.

Dr. Amit Ray is a mystic and spiritual master. He is author of several books on meditation and yoga. He did his PhD in computational neuroscience, worked as a scientist, had scientific patents and earned many other accolades. From his childhood, he learnt meditation from the wondering monks and ascetics who happened to pass by their village farmhouse. While he was working in a corporate job in London, many uncommon mystical experiences happened to him.

At the peak of his fame and thriving career, to the astonishment of his friends and colleagues, he decided to leave his career and high profile job in USA to commit his life for the search of ultimate truth. With a scientific bent of mind, he undertook meditation practices of Hindu and Buddhist tradition, without being entangled in the dogmatic views and rituals. With his wife, friend and spiritual companion Banani, he pursued a dedicated search for the truth in their cottage on the high mountain in a Himalayan village, undergoing intense spiritual practices of deep meditation and silence. He experienced a series of powerful and profound awakening, which revealed to him the true nature of human reality and existence. Realizing the liberating truth, he began to live and share his wisdom.

Also from Inner Light Publishers

Om Chanting and Meditation by Amit Ray

Om is our blissful Self. Om is the mysterious cosmic energy that is the substratum of all the things and all the beings. It is the eternal song of the Divine. This book makes the Om meditation easy to follow, simple to do, and very effective.

ISBN: 9788191026931

Glory of OM: A Journey to Self-Realization - A Modern Commentary on Mandukya Upanishad – by Banani Ray

The book explores the glory of Om in the context of self-realization. This book is a modern commentary of the ancient text Mandukya Upanishad. In all ages, evolved human minds have never ceased to wander about their own Self. Who am I? Why do we exist on earth? What is the purpose of this life and what happens after death? Does God really exist? Such questions have forever haunted seekers in all cultures and religions of the world. In the light of Mandukya Upanishad , this book addresses such questions that hang around the mind of a seeker of Self-realization.

Laughing Buddha: The Alchemy of Euphoric Living by Sakshi Chetana

The spirit of Laughing Buddha is the spirit of ultimate relaxation, happiness and contentment. This book gives a rare combination of ancient Buddhist wisdom and its practical use in our daily lives in the modern world for living in joy. ISBN: 9788191026948

Inner Light Publishers are dedicated to publishing books that helps improve the quality of human lives. You are welcome to visit us at www.inner-light-in.com.

Made in the USA
Monee, IL
25 May 2023

34561553R00135